Step Into Your Miracle

SHANNON MICHELLE

Liberté Press books may be purchased for educational, business, or sales promotional use. For information, please email the Special Markets Department at info@libertepress.com

NONFICTION / Memoir / Trauma / Traumatic Brain Injury / Breast Cancer

Library of Congress Control Number: 2024948099

libertepress.com | ISBN 979-8-9909388-1-6 (paperback) | First Edition

TRAUMA TRIGGER WARNING

This book contains content that may be distressing or triggering for some readers, especially survivors. Please be aware of the following themes and scenes:

- **Severe Motorcycle Accident:** Detailed descriptions of a motorcycle accident and its aftermath.
- **Medical Procedures:** Graphic depictions of surgeries and treatments, including those related to breast cancer.
- **Mental Health:** In-depth accounts of mental health struggles, such as depression and anxiety.
- **Sexual Assault:** Explicit descriptions of sexual assault and its emotional and physical impact.
- **Alcoholism:** Narratives involving alcoholism and its effects on individuals and families.
- **Child Abuse:** Depictions of child abuse and its lasting trauma. Please take care while reading. Your well-being is important.

Illustration by Grace Reason
Front Cover design by Liz Blume
Book design by Liz Blume
Edited by Karen Smith
Executive Producer Teresa Rodriguez

Liberté Press San Francisco
558 Presidio Blvd. Suite B, # 29015
San Francisco, CA 94129-5710

Liberté Press New York
521 Jerusalem Ave.
N. Belmore, NY 11710

Step Into Your Miracle

SHANNON MICHELLE

LIBERTÉ
PRESS

DEDICATION
For Grace

CONTENTS

IN GRATITUDE

First and foremost, to Grace, my anchor and the reason I continue to grow. My heart is full of gratitude for you. From being your protector to you becoming mine, we have navigated through life together, each taking turns to guide the other.

To Jessica and Dana, you have been my pillars of support and resilience, balancing my recovery both mentally and physically. Your strength has been my strength.

Mom, I love you so big. Thank you for bringing me into this crazy world.

Uncle Steve, you are one of the smartest and kindest men I know. Thank you for always being there.

To Brian, thank you for showing up in this time of trauma. You have been a true gentleman and an amazing father to our daughter Grace.

To my true, core friends who were at my side during those dark moments, I am forever grateful to you for holding my hand and wiping my ass.

To those engaging friends who read the manuscript and provided honest feedback, your candid insights and unwavering friendship have been invaluable.

The Newman family, you have shown up for me with such strength, kindness, and consistency.

And to my ex-partners—lovers and friends alike—I extend my gratitude. Thank you for the lessons learned and for not showing up. Your departures have made space for new beginnings.

Finally, to Teresa, a profoundly smart, insightful, and inspiring person. Your guidance has given me the courage and ability to share my story with the world.

Thank you all for being part of this incredible journey.

I share my story with you in hopes that you don't have to go through a literal wreck like I did to discover a place of peaceful living. Through this massive change, I gained some priceless gifts, helping me walk through my life with more clarity and satisfaction than I have ever experienced. I'm not going to lie, my healing process sucked, but I wouldn't change a thing because I am now a human being instead of a human doing.

– Shannon Michelle

" What we call darkness and pain are of value. If we pay attention to their lessons, they can help us grow and evolve. Our light doesn't shun the darkness. It embraces it and transforms it into a gift. "

— Shannon Michelle

breaking

The glassblower knows: while in the heat of beginning, any shape is possible. Once hardened, the only way to change is to break.

– Mark Nepo, *The Book of Awakening*

SUNDAYS WERE MY FAVORITE DAY OF THE WEEK. I spent the afternoons cruising on my motorcycle with close friends and fellow riders. Each week, we would take a different road trip. Some Sundays, we ventured into the Los Angeles hills, stopping for lunch at a quaint restaurant in the woods. Other times, we headed north, up the Pacific Coast Highway. Those were always my favorite rides. I felt such a connection with water and the ocean. Even with my helmet on, I could smell the fresh sea breeze and feel the sun's warmth on my body. The sound of my Harley-Davidson® motorcycle revving when I accelerated sent waves of joy through my body. I found freedom in riding.

The theme of my life has been freedom and safety. I had a tough childhood which left me in a perpetual state of uncertainty and fear. For many years, I didn't know where home was going to be, and when I did, many times, it was filled with all types of abuse. Growing up in a chaotic environment fueled my drive to build a secure sanctuary when I finally left home. Creating a cozy nest where I could feel at ease became my mission, stemming from my yearning for comfort and stability. My dedication to designing interiors for others arose from a profound personal desire and necessity. Before becoming a highly respected interior designer, I would refurbish old furniture, taking something old and worn and giving it a new, beautiful life. Although I didn't attend college, I was gifted with an eye for design and style. I was a clever businesswoman, and by my mid-twenties, I opened a few successful retail boutiques in Los Angeles and Santa Monica. My creations caught the eye of a famous actor who invested in my dream and helped me open my second boutique.

Another blessing was when I got pregnant. I made a commitment: my daughter's life would be the complete opposite of the train wreck that was my youth. Being a single mom, I was determined to create a better life for my daughter than I had. This determination drove every decision, propelling me to become a successful entrepreneur with an impressive interior design empire. Despite the challenges, including long nights working with demanding, high-net-worth clients and celebrities and managing a hectic schedule, I never lost sight of that goal: a happier, more secure future. My efforts to build a strong foundation for us both were fueled by the hope for a life far removed from the uncertainties and fears of my own childhood.

Like many women, I clung to society's definition of a successful woman. I dressed right, my hair and makeup were always on point, and my social calendar was a buzz of activity. Sure, I had my fair share of therapy sessions, but there was a part of me that didn't dive too deeply into what I truly needed. I neglected my own well-being, and it was time to prioritize self-care and introspection.

So, when my daughter left for college, I felt a sense of ease. For the first time in my life, I was finally living for myself. The transition was bittersweet, but the newfound independence was invigorating. For the first time in decades, my days weren't dictated by school schedules, extracurricular activities, or driving my daughter and her friends around Los Angeles. I rediscovered hobbies shelved for years and even took spontaneous road trips on my motorcycle to places I'd bookmarked but never visited. Once a daunting prospect, the silence of the house transformed into peaceful solace, offering me uninterrupted hours to read, meditate, and simply be with my thoughts. This chapter of life, while initially daunting, became a period of self-discovery and personal growth. However, that era of freedom and adventure was about to end abruptly and painfully.

On Sunday, February 6, 2022, our pack of riders embarked on a scenic adventure up the Pacific Coast Highway. We toured the winding roads in Malibu and stopped at a Mexican restaurant for lunch. We headed back south as the sun stretched its rays over the Southern California coastline. While the rest of the riders wanted to explore Malibu Canyon, I rode south down the Pacific Coast Highway to meet my friends, Jen and Ted, who were driving down from San Luis Obispo.

Ted had been diagnosed with cancer and needed to be at UCLA, and I told them they could stay with me. The plan was that I would meet them at my house that Sunday afternoon. They decided to take the scenic route down the Pacific Coast Highway, but unfortunately, were caught in a serious accident in Malibu and didn't get to my house until much later. As for me, I didn't return home for months.

Although I have no recollection of colliding with the vehicle that performed an illegal U-turn in front of me, the police report states that when they pulled out into the highway at a perpendicular angle to the road, my motorcycle slammed into the front driver's side of the vehicle, traveling thirty-five miles per hour. When my bike hit the car, the front wheel and handlebars crumpled under the sheer force. Both my wrists were shattered on impact, along with my pelvis. Witnesses say that I was thrown thirty feet into the air. My beloved Harley-Davidson rolled across the highway in pieces, and I slammed hard on the asphalt. When I crashed into the black tarmac, headfirst, motorcycle parts, fluids, lights, and glass scattered into oncoming traffic. I rolled across the highway like a wet towel.

Unconscious and clad in leather, I battled severe internal bleeding and suffered from multiple fractures throughout my body. Witnesses said that a man, who was also a motorcycle enthusiast, parked his car in front of my body and directed traffic around what looked like a leather-clad rag doll, making sure no one drove over me on the usually fast highway. An off-duty EMT enjoying the beach ran to the scene, checked my vitals, and called for a medevac because he knew I was on the verge of death.

I was flown to UCLA via LA County Fire Department helicopter, where the emergency room staff fought to save my life. I remained unconscious and unaware of what had happened to me. Details of that critical time remain elusive to everyone, since the medical staff had no way of notifying my next of kin about the accident. What set off the alarm was that my friend, Lee, with whom I'd been riding that day, returned to my house only to find it dark with no sign of me. Lee called Jen and Ted, expecting I was having dinner with them, but they were still stuck on the highway. Lee tried calling me, but I didn't pick up. Once Jen and Ted arrived at my house with Lee, they called the police and every hospital in Los

"At 4:30 in the morning, my daughter and I found ourselves at the UCLA Trauma Center. The room was eerily quiet as we stood before Shannon's motionless body, surrounded by tubes and machines. The only sounds were the beeps of her heart monitor and the whirring of the life-saving equipment. It was a surreal and unforgettable moment that I never hope to relive."

— Brian Reason, Shannon's ex, and father of their daughter

Angeles. Finally, they learned that I was unconscious and in critical condition.

First, they called Brian, my ex and the father of my daughter, informing him of my accident. Brian was told that he had to call the hospital immediately because it was a matter of life and death. In shock, he spoke to the doctors and received the grave news that they didn't know if I would make it through the night. Once off the phone, he drove straight to our daughter's university. It was a three-hour drive to pick her up and tell her the news and another three hours back to UCLA's intensive care unit where I lay fighting for my life.

I was in a coma for around two months, which was probably a good thing since my body took a beating. I underwent a tracheostomy procedure while unconscious to aid my breathing. A percutaneous endoscopic gastrostomy tube was inserted into my stomach to feed my motionless body. I experienced a closed traumatic brain injury that caused severe brain swelling. Severe internal bleeding and swelling in my right eye paralyzed the nerve responsible for its outward movement, leaving me cross-eyed. Hemorrhaging behind my left eye also caused some nerve damage. Tubes placed in my skull relieved the pressure in my head.

My traumatic brain injuries left everyone uncertain about my recovery. Would I regain full consciousness? And if so, could I resume life as a fully functioning adult, or would I require 24-7 care?

After numerous x-rays and an exploratory laparotomy—that's when they cut you open to see what's going on in your abdomen—they found my pelvis in pieces. So, they searched for the bone fragments and put them back together with screws and metal plates.

The doctors were confident in the surgeries they performed to put my pelvis back together, but there still a chance I would lose the use of my right hand. Of all the trauma I experienced, the most

" While I lay in ICU, my family and friends gathered around me, waiting to hear any news from the doctors. Although my cognitive recovery was still a mystery, the doctors did know that I had shattered both wrists to the point that the use of my hands was jeopardized. "

– Shannon Michelle

frightening for all was happening under my skull. The mystery surrounding brain damage left everyone in suspense. Due to my unconscious state and the severity of the accident, the possibility of neurological damage was high.

Some of the chronic physical damages that concerned the doctors included:

- Slurred speech
- Headaches
- Blurred/double vision
- Convulsions/seizures
- Nausea/vomiting
- Weakness in extremities or face
- Loss of balance.

Some of the cognitive or behavioral issues that I could suffer included:

- Confusion or disorientation
- Struggles with my memory, concentration, or decision-making
- Loss of consciousness or change in consciousness
- Having trouble waking up or experiencing a decreased level of consciousness
- Feeling increased frustration or irritability
- Changes in my sleep patterns, like increased sleep, difficulty waking up, restlessness, or trouble falling/staying asleep.

Other issues would include perception and sensation:

- Feelings of increased fatigue and drowsiness
- Decreased energy levels and motivation
- Sensitivity to light or sound
- Unpleasant taste in my mouth
- Difficulty hearing or ringing in my ears

- Light-headedness, dizziness, vertigo, and difficulty with balance and coordination
- Feeling anxious or depressed
- Mood changes, including mood swings, combativeness, agitation, or other unusual behavior.

These questions about my mental health and physical abilities could not be answered until I woke from my coma. But, before that would happen, I would leave my body and enter an ethereal place between life and death. My healing journey would involve more than learning to walk or speak again; it entailed relearning what it meant to live, love, and let go.

"The doctors said that they didn't know how Shannon would recover from this awful accident. She could not wake up. She could end up brain-dead. They didn't know if she would be able to talk or even care for herself. They didn't know what kind of person would return to us if Shannon did wake. The doctors were not very hopeful. So, it was her friends and family who kept up hope."

– L.P., Shannon's close friend and riding buddy

floating

Out beyond ideas of wrongdoing and right-doing, there is a field. I'll meet you there.

– Rumi

THE FIRST RESPONDERS WHO CAREFULLY SCRAPED me off the highway were so traumatized by my condition that the captain sent them home. Thankfully, I escaped the gruesome vision of my broken body because my consciousness began its journey to a place between time and space. It was there that I encountered a host of entities and friends who would help me on the painful journey back into my body. One of the most important people who met me was someone I considered my father figure, but who had died eight months earlier.

His obituary read: "William (Bill) Charles Langford, Jr., died on Friday, May 28, 2021, in Lafayette after a fierce battle with brain cancer." But when I last saw him, he was quite alive and well. For nearly two decades, Bill represented what a father was meant to be. He was safe, loving, generous, and wise. I met him through one of my best friends, Dana. She lived in Los Angeles, but was originally from Lafayette, Louisiana. When she decided to return home, she invited me to visit, and I fell in love with their pastoral property. Their home, vibrant with life and lush greenery, became a sanctuary for my daughter, Grace, and me. With his open arms and warm, tender smile, Bill was the embodiment of what a father should be.

Over two decades, our visits became a cherished ritual, surrounding us in the warm embrace of the Langford family's rich tapestry of traditions and celebrations. During lazy days spent under the expansive Louisiana sky, Bill taught Grace and me invaluable lessons about life, family, and the bonds that intertwine with us.

Bill and his wife, Mary, spent many seasons in Haiti doing mission work through their church and invited me one year. The trip changed my life. I gained a new appreciation for service and admiration for Bill and Mary. Along with volunteering in Haiti and involvement with their church community, Bill and Mary offered equine therapy for children and veterans. Bill was a pillar of his community and the beloved patriarch of his family, so when he died of brain cancer, the loss of such a great man shocked everyone in his community. I was with Bill's family when he passed, and little did I know that I would be face-to-face with him where he would be more alive than ever.

While my physical body was on the verge of shutting down and dying, I was fully alive and very aware of what was happening to me, even though I wasn't physically in my body. My first memory when I woke into this new consciousness was seeing balloons floating in a bright, blue sky teeming with fluffy clouds. The air was soft and warm, yet misty. Before me, I heard a beautiful angel repeating, "You. You. You." At first, I was scared because I didn't know where I was. Then this overwhelming sense of peace engulfed me, and I rested in that present moment. There was no other place I wanted to be.

So many beautiful, light entities surrounded me, and I kept hearing, "You got this! You got this! You got this!" They kept telling me that I wasn't alone and that they had me in their care. As I floated, I felt Bill beside me, his calming spirit showing me that everything would be OK. His presence held and supported me. He patted my shoulder, repeating, "It's OK, it's OK, it's OK."

I felt an angel named Rebecca with me. She comforted me. I kept hearing, "You are never alone. We're here, and you are never alone." During this time, a sense of light filled my consciousness, and I felt like a happy child just wanting to giggle. Together, we all began to laugh. I was floating above the life I knew, and I was so joyful and carefree. Then I looked down to where my body lay, and the light began to fade slowly. I felt small, and the darkness took over. I could feel the sticky weight of my body. It felt like a cold, wet coat laid across me.

I felt another angel named James near me. He reminded me that the darkness is OK as well. He told me: "Step into your darkness. It's going to be OK. We got you. It's going to be OK." At that moment, I knew I was balancing between life and death and being drawn into the light. I could feel the pain and heaviness of my ruined body, and I didn't want to go back into that broken shell tied down with tubes and casts. Then, I saw a door before me. I was breathing hard, and I was scared. I pushed the door open, and there was so much light that I began hyperventilating. The pain in my head

" Step into your darkness.
It's going to be OK.
We got you.
It's going to be OK. **"**

– Shannon Michelle

was pounding, and I yelled, "Release my head! Please let go of my head!"

There was a strong urge to enter the light because I knew there was no pain and only joy in its warm, eternal glow. I floated forward to it and began coughing because I couldn't breathe. I wanted release from the pain, and I wanted to be able to breathe freely and go into that radiance filled with peace and white light.

I floated toward the door with Bill by my side. Countless angels surrounded Bill and me. I had this sensation of Bill holding my hand and allowing me to stay in this space between life and death. In his kind, baritone voice, he told me, "I know it's messy, right?"

All I could do was look up and feel the effervescent joy of what was beyond the door. That was where I wanted to be. I couldn't look down to the pain and heaviness waiting for me back on earth. Bill held my hand so I could stay present enough to understand what I would be leaving if I didn't return to my shattered body. I remember hovering between two different spaces, like swimming where the cold ocean meets the warm water of a gentle river. One direction felt like a stream of joy and freedom, while the other felt like a murky abyss of heaviness and misery. It was so dark and dense, reminding me what I would return to if I reentered my body.

If I floated into this joyous place filled with light, I would leave my daughter, my friends, and all those people I'd help by sharing my profound journey. If I came back, I would have to suffer through all the damage that my body endured. I hesitated. Did I really want to go back into that awful mound of flesh I didn't recognize? Where was that smiling, energetic, healthy person I was before the accident? It took me a long time to decide to return to the trauma and sadness of my earthly mess. Still, Bill held my hand, letting me know it would all be OK.

Without Bill's reassuring presence, I may have drifted toward the light, leaving behind my earthly existence. His unwavering support was all that anchored me to my fragile body in the hospital. Bill's connection brought me a sense of security. So, I slowly agreed to return, knowing that when I did, I would no longer be the same person I was before my accident. The uncertainty of that truth was profound.

Before returning, I spent a few weeks in a coma, floating in the space between, redefining my life on a deep and spiritual level. If someone had told me the Sunday morning of my accident that my personality, values, and mannerisms were going to change dramatically, I would have given them a mischievous smile while whispering, "Bullshit."

I had to have this out-of-body experience because I was getting downloaded, trained, and upgraded from the person I was before. The trauma I experienced was a crucial turning point for my personal development. This experience taught me to trust in a higher power to heal my body and mind. I was given a rare and priceless glimpse into the divine. I learned that we are all connected, loved, and given the grace to make our own choices.

While my friends and family held vigils over my motionless body, hoping that I would regain consciousness, I was out there doing some major work. I did return, but not as the same person I was before my accident. Although my friends and family celebrated when I woke from my coma, most were shocked to meet the new Shannon 2.0.

changing

When we are no longer able to change a situation—we are challenged to change ourselves.

– Viktor E. Frankl

BEFORE MY ACCIDENT, MY LIFE APPEARED INCREDIBLY well-managed and quite successful. I took pride in my hard work and ability to make my clients' seemingly impossible dreams come true. My friends, family, and clients assumed I could do everything. From a distance, it looked like I accomplished everything effortlessly and gracefully. When I stepped out for the day, I made sure that my outfits were on point, along with my hair and light makeup.

The image I gave the world was one of "Boss Mom" ready to take on any challenge. To my friends, I was their touchstone; to my clients, I was their problem solver; to my family, I was their feathered nest. When something went south or if someone needed a helping hand, I was always there for them, no questions asked. I prided myself on my calm yet assertive demeanor and ability to get shit done.

Ironically, the narrative I showed to the world differed from the fears and insecurities banging around in my head. My well-controlled mannerisms and glossy exterior gave no hint of self-doubt. But lurking behind the veiled curtain of my extraordinary life, my inner limiting beliefs and weaknesses stopped me from living a truly authentic life. Because of my traumatic childhood, I kept up my guard and was highly protective around new people. As a child of sexual abuse and single mom, I was always afraid that something could happen to my daughter. And when it came to men, I easily found faults and loopholes in my relationships. The diehard cynic in me refused to let down my walls or show my vulnerabilities.

Like so many others, especially mothers and women who have suffered from abuse, I kept calm and carried on, regardless of the storms brewing inside. My whole life, I solved problems and helped others, but I could never ask for help, share my vulnerabilities, or admit that I needed support.

Pre-crash, I was caught up in making sure my adult life was better than the burning heap of my childhood. I got very good at shutting down the bad shit, so that I could get through my days. I didn't know how to share my tragedies or sorrows, nor did I want to. I struggled to show my vulnerabilities because, to me, that was admitting weakness. Reflecting on my past, it's clear why I was a talented designer. I knew how to transform challenging rooms into stunning living spaces.

" We all connect to each other
and to the universe on our own
channels. We might describe it
differently, but at the heart of it,
we all reflect our oneness. "

—Shannon Michelle

One critical aspect of this experience was gaining a new level of fearlessness and courage. I believe this accident and the following experiences I had during my recovery were essential parts of my growth. As much as it sucked, the pain and trauma of my accident served as a crucial turning point for my personal development.

This transformation was intensely physical, mental, and spiritual. I learned the importance of slowing down, listening to my body, and being present in each moment. It was a stark departure from my previous lifestyle in which the emphasis was always on doing more, achieving more, and never truly resting. Through this healing process, I discovered the power of mindfulness, the strength in vulnerability, and the peace that comes from genuinely connecting with oneself. It was as though I were learning to breathe anew, to see the world through lenses tinted with gratitude and wonder rather than through the gray hues of relentless productivity.

One of the most significant steps in my journey was learning to open up and ask for help. I had to become comfortable with receiving support, not just giving it. It was crucial to accept help kindly and acknowledge that it's OK to be needy. It's not about being the stereotypically "needy" person, but understanding that needing help is part of being human. Embracing my vulnerability and brokenness was essential. I had to allow others to take control at times, which was a significant shift for me, as I was so used to steering my own course.

I used to think that vulnerability was a sign of weakness. However, I've come to understand that vulnerability is as beautiful and kind as love. It is a gift, not something to be feared or seen as a negative trait. This realization was a significant shift for me. The word that resonates with me is grace, particularly in the context of my relationship with my daughter. I needed to be honorable and stay present with my brokenness and past traumas. In the past, I couldn't let anyone in; I couldn't be vulnerable with my previous brokenness. I mistakenly thought that if people knew the "real me" and my chaotic past, then they wouldn't see me as perfect and wonderfully made. So, I hid my true self to stay protected from judgment and rejection. Yet, I should not have done the very act of hiding. Vulnerability was not something to shield myself from but to embrace.

Shannon 1.0 struggled with her emotions. I often went back to the same patterns, masking my true feelings. In the past, I showed up emotionally and physically as if everything were OK, even when it wasn't. I put on a façade, presenting myself as being just fine to everyone around me. This façade was a form of limitation, preventing me from fully showing up and being authentic.

I used to think trauma was purely negative, something to avoid. Bad things happening were just that—bad. I wanted no part in them. However, I've learned that embracing rather than hiding from these experiences allows for growth. Accepting and moving beyond the trauma doesn't diminish it; instead, it becomes a part of my journey toward personal development.

Reflecting on my past, I realize most of it felt chaotic. My childhood and early twenties were tumultuous times that shaped who I became. I wrestled with not wanting to replicate the environment I came from. I was determined not to become an alcoholic, not to be abusive, and not to make poor financial decisions like my mother. She taught me how to pretend to show up, always looking good on the surface. I didn't want to be what I had been shown.

But that's all in the past now. I've come to understand that, while I am a product of my past, I am not defined by it. I can look forward to the future and build something better. I've found a path to personal growth and fulfillment by overcoming my history and embracing my true self.

While in a coma, I discovered these incredible skills. It would have taken me years to understand and practice these teachings. I am grateful that I was in a coma, allowing the divine to communicate these immutable truths to me. However, I had to overcome some dramatic physical, mental, and emotional hurdles before I could share them with the world.

waking

You're on an incredible healing journey that no one expected. Remember your journey, and don't worry about what you've forgotten. Just keep staying present.

– Shannon Michelle

TWO LONG MONTHS AFTER MY ACCIDENT, I WAS moved into a nursing home to begin the rehabilitation journey. Returning to consciousness was like being reborn, thrust into a reality where I had to relearn the basics of living. My wrists were in casts, my pelvis was still healing, and I had lost all control over my bodily functions. I couldn't eat or go to the bathroom without assistance. Walking was impossible. I went in and out of consciousness. In those moments, I was a stranger to myself, wrestling with the parts of a life I couldn't remember. Each time my mind rebooted, I struggled to adjust to my new reality which I didn't understand.

One of my earliest memories involves waking up or, rather, repeatedly drifting into consciousness, only to find myself in a haze of confusion and disorientation. I was convinced I was in New Orleans each time I opened my eyes. The idea of being in California was a concept my mind couldn't grasp.

"Where am I? Where am I?" The question echoed nonstop. Every time I asked, the answer felt out of reach. My vision was blurred and hazy due to nerve damage around my eyes, making everything unfamiliar. I could only repeatedly ask, "Am I in New Orleans?"

New Orleans was the last trip I took just days before my accident, so I think that's why my brain went there. Every moment was like waking up in an unfamiliar city after a long trip, disoriented and jet-lagged. But it was happening over and over again while I was awake.

The struggle to piece together my surroundings was awful. I tried to remember how and why I ended up immobile, in pain, and in a nursing home. The worst part was my complete lack of memory. I had no past to cling to, no anchor to ground me. Imagine a table covered with puzzle pieces but no photo of what the puzzle is supposed to look like. Then, adding to the confusion, most of the puzzle pieces were missing or damaged.

This cycle of waking and questioning seemed endless, each episode of consciousness followed by a relapse into darkness. Time became an abstract concept, so I tried to hold onto my location. It took weeks before the realization stuck with me: I was in California. This truth was something I had to relearn repeatedly.

The weeks before my awakening in the nursing home were completely erased from my memory. I have no memory of being at UCLA and Kaiser, even though everyone told me I was there. My return to consciousness began in the nursing hospital, and I had zero recollection of the two other hospitals I was in for months.

Others might tell a different story. They have videos of me looking alert and responsive. But I was far from conscious. I wasn't truly back. My memory holds no trace of those earlier days. It's as if I were living in a state of suspended animation, where my body was present but my ability to remember each passing moment was blank. I couldn't hold onto anything that happened. People told me that I repeated the same thing over and over again, but I didn't know I was doing that.

Besides the light coming in through the window, I had no sense of time. I had no idea how long I had been somewhere or how long I had felt a certain way. I could barely figure out what my body wanted or needed, and the moment I did, I would disappear into the fog again.

Despite what others saw or believed, my recovery was a gradual process of piecing my life together, one fragment at a time. It felt like I was stuck in a loop, a never-ending cycle of confusion and frustration, not understanding my limitations or the trauma that my body suffered. I was told that my brain hit the pavement at forty-five miles per hour, so no wonder I was left with a limited capacity to process my surroundings.

Throughout my journey of recovery, one theme remained constant: chaos. I was in a state of perpetual disarray, trying to gather the pieces of my shattered reality. My friends told me that I tried to get out of bed alone and walk to the bathroom. I didn't remember that my pelvis was shattered and held together with rods and wires. I thought I could stand up and walk as if sheer willpower could undo the damage.

I was determined to get out of bed, unaware of the full extent of my limitations and injuries. The strength I felt in my legs gave me

> " I would wake up in that nursing hospital over and over again, and I kept wondering, where the fuck am I?
>
> – Shannon Michelle

false hope that I could stand and walk, even though my arms were immobilized in casts. My relentless attempts to rise led the nurses to restrain me, preventing any further harm.

"Where am I? How do I escape this? Why is it happening?" Then, the questions would start all over again.

When I started getting more aware of my awful predicament, I would wake up in a state of overwhelming fear, unsure of who I was or what had happened. It felt like my entire sense of self had evaporated, and I didn't even know who I was before the accident. I didn't know who I was from moment to moment. Questions swirled in my mind: What happened? How am I supposed to understand this? I had no reference points to ground me, no familiar markers to guide me back to safety.

My whole life, I prided myself on controlling my fears, desires, and actions. I avoided drinking too much because I didn't like the sensation of losing control. I carefully monitored my words to ensure I never offended anyone. I thrived within the boundaries of the safe, predictable world I had meticulously crafted for myself.

I managed my life with calculated caution and steady self-assurance. Yet here I was, waking up in a disorienting fog, unable to remember who I was or where I was. The very foundation of my existence seemed to have crumbled beneath me.

Although the breathing tube had been removed, a feeding tube still snaked its way into my body since I was in a coma. One day, I tried to pull the tube out, since I had no idea what it was or why it was in my body. I managed to dislodge it just enough for the liquid inside to seep into my body, adding another layer of discomfort to my already disoriented state.

I was told that the liquid "nutrition formula" dripped into my abdominal cavity. I went into septic shock, and my organs began to shut down. I was rushed into surgery, where two liters of rancid

> " Finding my memory was elusive. It would float away and then would return like a soft breeze. Then, it would drift away into a dream. But this was all happening while I was awake. "

— Shannon Michelle

fluid were removed from my swollen body. So, along with all the other scars from the motorcycle accident, I also have a huge one across my belly from the feeding tube debacle. I don't remember this happening, but I do have the scar to remind me. It's another sign on the road map of my life's journey.

When I gained consciousness, I was given food to eat but had to figure out what to do with it. The doctors worried that I wouldn't remember how to eat or, when I did eat, that I would forget what I ate, so the feeding tube remained.

Finally, I was given my phone, but I needed to figure out what it was and how to use it. I started taking photos of my food to show the nurses that I did, in fact, eat.

Along with losing my mind and bodily functions, I lost my long red locks of hair. Following several procedures involving stents placed in my skull to alleviate brain pressure, my scalp became a tangled mess, smeared with dried blood. After the stents were removed, my friends gently broached the subject of shaving my hair, making sure they got my approval multiple times, ensuring I fully understood and agreed. I agreed. Once again, another part of my identity was shaved away.

Consistently doubting myself, I found solace in my phone. It was a faithful memory companion, capturing and reminding me of moments I might otherwise lose in the fog of forgetfulness. The simple act of taking a photo became an anchor to my experiences. Each photo was a way to remember, show, and prove that these moments were real—that my life was real. The camera wasn't just capturing images; it was capturing my existence, piece by piece.

When my mind felt wiped clean, like a computer rebooted and struggling to reload, my phone bridged the gap. It served as an external hard drive for my brain, storing the fragments of my past that I could no longer hold onto myself. Every image taken

" The best way I can describe the feeling is that my mind felt like a computer that had been completely wiped clean. It was as if all my memories had been deleted. Each slight recollection triggered the next memory, slowly piecing my life back together, bit by bit. "

– Shannon Michelle

was a pixel in the larger picture of my life, a proof of my continual journey.

I often found myself scrolling through my camera, revisiting the photos I had taken during various stages of my life. Each image was a key, unlocking memories buried deep within me. Seeing these snapshots allowed my brain to reconnect with some of those moments, helping me piece together the narrative of my days.

Using my phone this way was more than just a coping mechanism; it was a means of reclaiming my identity. The photos offered a sense of continuity, a way to trace the threads of my story back to their origins. In those captured moments, I found the proof I needed to believe in my own experiences and see my progress despite the challenges of memory loss.

I frequently looked at my phone to know what day it was or to confirm if it was still the same day. I remember relying on my phone often or asking others what day of the week it was. Eventually, I reached a point where I cared about knowing the day of the week. Previously, the day of the week never made sense to me because every day felt like an endless cycle of repetition.

In those early days, I found myself continually resetting, trying to anchor myself in reality. I'd take pictures to prove something had happened because writing was still beyond me. It wasn't until recently that I began to read again. It has been a frustrating process of baby steps, slowly relearning words and their meanings. Now, I'm much better. I can read at a basic level, a vast improvement from where I started. I'd "write" by talking into my phone and recording it.

To anyone struggling with similar battles, know that it's OK to lean on tools and technologies that help you navigate the complexities of your mind. Embrace the aids that allow you to hold onto your memories, for they are the bridges that connect us to ourselves and the world around us.

While I could talk, finding the right words was very difficult. I wasn't aware enough to think about finishing a sentence; my mind didn't go that deep. When I spoke, it was slow and difficult. Each word felt like it had to be pulled from a dense fog. Often, my speech made little sense.

What stands out most vividly are people's questions: "Do you remember me? Do you know my name?" It's a peculiar sensation, being confronted with faces that should be familiar but aren't, like pages torn out of a book you've read a thousand times. I would wave, smile, and nod as if to say, "Of course, I know who you are." But in reality, the answer was often, "No, I have no idea who you are." This scenario repeated itself a lot. What struck me most was how safe and familiar some people felt.

The first sense to return was touch. It wasn't the words or sounds that made me recognize them; it was their touch and the feelings that evoked. The emotional connections remained intact even when the verbal cues were lost.

There were people I had known for as long as I could remember—or so I was told—who had become strangers in the vast, empty landscape of my mind. The abyss of forgotten memories had swallowed their names and faces. It was so frustrating for everyone, especially me.

Some people visited me during my hospital stay and later told me, "I came to visit you. Do you remember?" To my surprise, I didn't remember. On the other hand, there were others whose presence was distinct in my mind. I could clearly remember them sitting next to me; their faces and actions were imprinted in my memory. It's significant to me that I didn't remember certain longtime friends and family members visiting. It feels like a big deal.

" In the end, these pictures are more than just images—they are the tangible evidence of a life lived, a testament to resilience, and a powerful reminder that even amid the haze of forgetfulness, we are still here, making memories one snapshot at a time. "

– Shannon Michelle

One vivid memory I do have is of my daughter, Grace. I don't know how I remembered her name, but I remember how she felt and the comfort she brought me.

My waking state was filled with pain and fear, except for the times when people I loved were near. Those moments felt safe, loving, and good. Otherwise, everything was scary, challenging, and painful. Tasks were complex, memories were difficult to retain, and physical activities were impossible to manage.

My friends and family hesitated to take pictures or videos of me during this time. They thought I would hate to see myself in that awful condition. They believed if they took pictures and recordings, I would not want people to see me that way. But now, I wish they had. I am an open book today, and I understand that they made those decisions to care for me in the best way they knew how under those extreme circumstances. They thought, "She will kill us if we take photos of her looking like hell."

Music has always been my passion.

During my time in a coma, the sound of music surrounded me, especially the tunes of Amos Lee whom I adored.

There's a video of me singing along with my daughter, a moment I don't recall but am grateful that my friends captured.

Before my accident, I was always on the move, living an active and fulfilling life. But everything changed when I woke up, and I could barely move. My right hand was entirely unusable. The bones in my wrist shattered beyond repair. The pain on my right side was so overwhelming that I had no choice but to relearn how to use my left hand. Simple tasks like lifting an object or reaching out to touch someone became painful challenges.

I know this is terrible, but the reality of having to pee and poo in a diaper at my age was something I vividly remember. It was humiliating and frustrating, and although my friends were supportive,

" This thing we call "memory" is not just about piecing together fragments of our past; it's a journey of self-discovery. It's about understanding the fluid nature of memory and coming to terms with the parts of our lives that have faded away. It's an exploration for those who seek to understand themselves through the lens of what they remember—and what they don't. "

– Shannon Michelle

it didn't help much. I often found myself relying on their assistance for even the simplest tasks.

There were countless occasions when I couldn't get to the toilet by myself. Physically, it was impossible. I'd have to press a buzzer, and someone would come to help me. Initially, they'd place a portable potty under me because I couldn't walk or get out of bed. This process was a stark reminder of my limitations, but it also made me set a goal: I wanted to regain my independence and get myself to the toilet without help.

Relearning bladder and bowel control became a crucial achievement I set out to accomplish independently. As an adult, you learn to hold your bladder until you can find a bathroom. I had lost that ability altogether because of the severe nerve, tissue, and muscle damage in my pelvis and abdomen.

I remember setting small, achievable goals for myself. One of the primary goals was to learn how to use my opposite hand better. Another crucial aim was to communicate my need to use the bathroom and try to hold it until I got help. Although I had to wear diapers at home for a long time, I always kept sight of my goals.

I remember feeling proud to know when the nurses would change my diaper. I could position myself in a way that made the process easier and more comfortable. I developed a slight sense of timing based on their routines and actions. However, I couldn't grasp the bigger picture, like how long I had been in the nursing home.

Whenever anyone came to visit, I would want to hold their hand. I needed that physical connection because touch became so significant to me. Most of the caretakers were amazing and sweet, and they understood how much their touch meant to me. However, touch was also intertwined with pain during that period. When I recall those moments, I remember being in a lot of pain. Having a friend hold my left hand, even for a moment, would relieve some of that pain. It would soften the experience and distract me from the discomfort, which was incredibly helpful.

Reflecting on these moments now, I realize waking up from my coma and going through all the trauma was a pivotal point in my life's journey. It forced me to confront the limitations of the safety net I had so carefully woven. Fear, which I had always kept at bay, had finally caught up with me. In those moments of vulnerability, I began to understand that true strength comes not from avoiding my weaknesses and fears, but from facing them head-on and navigating through them.

This experience taught me that life's most remarkable transformations often come from terrifying moments. In these times of profound uncertainty and fear, we discover our deepest reserves of resilience and courage. As I continue to navigate this journey, I am learning to embrace the unknown, to let go of the need for total control, and to trust in the process of becoming.

sharing

Remain Suspicious of the idea of a fixed
identity.   – Shannon Michelle

IT CAN BE HARD TO RECOGNIZE YOUR PROGRESS
when you're still navigating the rough path of trauma recovery.
I understand that feeling completely. That's why I want to share a
part of my story when I started to wrestle my way out of the darkness.
To make this meaningful for your healing, I took the time to consult
with friends and read through hundreds of journal entries. My first
entry was spoken into my phone a few months after I woke up from
the coma. I couldn't read yet, but I learned how to record notes.

Perhaps you will see yourself in my struggles and realize that healing is a gradual process. You'll encounter a mix of turmoil and fear but also moments of joy and unexpected surprises. Throughout this process, I had to remind myself: Hang in there, you're making more progress than you know!

There's a lot to unpack in my journal entries. I get it if it's too much for you. While I believe there's a ton of insights and ah-ha moments you'll relate to, please take your time going through this section. I suggest that you absorb what resonates with you and feel free to move onto Chapter 6 whenever you're ready.

Some names have been changed for privacy. Also, I didn't want to fix the grammatical errors, so you can experience how wackadoodle my brain was. Sometimes, I didn't remember the right word, so I used the words I knew. This journal takes you on a journey that concludes two years after my accident.

JOURNAL ENTRIES

JULY 3, 2022
9:02 PM
Surprise! I've made it back into the world from a sad, death-filled experience over the past five months!
Yesterday was my first day back to the beach.
Slow, but possible recovery!

AUGUST 13, 2022
8:10 AM
Opposite of shame.
Fear and shame get in the way of relationships.

SEPTEMBER 22, 2022
7:56 PM
Therapy meeting.
How to process the large days at home.
Friends disappeared a bit more. I was sitting at the pool after I did my walk-swim... thought it's just like a vacation (but it's not).
Been working on making "to do" lists, but those go pretty quick; the rest of the day starts to feel empty.

OCTOBER 8, 2022
8:36 AM
Floating in the sky today.

DECEMBER 16, 2022
12:38 PM
I was sad on the phone.
Having her (Grace) here reminds me that I'm me. 💜 😀
I think that's something I don't understand.
Grace and I were laughing so hard that I felt like moments are coming back to me if I just hold onto each moment of growth, I tell myself.
Walk, read, rest...reset.

DECEMBER 18, 2022
10:50 AM
I am trying to remember who Shannon Michelle was.
This is what I'm remembering:
Mom divorced my father six months old.
Age we moved in with my father?
Age we moved Helena, Montana?
Age moved back to Southern California?
Age I had my first job on Huntington Dr. at Flicks liquor store?
Lived in an apartment with my mom and brother with a pool.
Summer between 10th and 11th grade when Mom made me move to my father's in Simi Valley. Lasted there for months, then moved in with my best friend in Simi Valley and her family.
Brian S., first real boyfriend, high school. He used to race cars.
Spiritual meeting...
Life gives us what we need at the moment we need it.

8:58 PM
It's so important to look back on your life, the good with the bad. Sometimes, we like to forget about the bad and move past it, but it's just as important to appreciate what you've been through as it is to experience the good.

DECEMBER 19, 2022
9:02 PM
Today is December 19, which seems to be enough time for all the anxiety, anxiousness, and pain to be gone by now. But that's not what happened. I had surgery for my neck and wrist the day before Thanksgiving. I knew that it wasn't going to be easy, but I had no idea how painful it would be a week later. This is more painful than the other surgery I remember on my wrist. One surgery, the doctors had to take out all the metal pieces. The metal was there so I wouldn't move it, but then they wanted my wrist to mend itself. I remember that surgery. I was able to get through it.

I know there were so many surgeries and moments of death-defying freedom that came back to my memory. My brain is coming back.

DECEMBER 21, 2022
6:01 AM
Relearning my life.
1975 Christmas shipped to live with my father.
1977 Moved to Helena, Montana with Mom.
1980 Summer back to California.
1982 Mom got sober. I was 13.
Spoke to my mom regarding memories of sexual abuse from my father and either R. or teacher from school. I had never asked her these questions. I hid it from her and everybody.

6:15 AM
Partly that was from the deepest place that I was not knowing how to forgive the "other woman." The one that scarred me the most was with my stepmother. She was the first "other woman." We had been shipped off to live with my father and his new wife and two children because my mom put herself in a mental hospital. That was the safest place for her. My stepmother was a super abuser. She used to lock me up in the closet and tell me to stop crying. She wouldn't let me out until I stopped. That never made sense to me. I learned (thought) at a very young age that I was not very likable.

There was a big oak tree on the block, and my favorite thing to do was climb to the top. Climbing the tree taught me that I was strong at a young age.

My memories aren't clear, but somebody came into my room and would feel me up and put my hands/body where they were not supposed to be. I remember telling my brother that I can't be here anymore, and I was going to ride my bike to Palm Springs because I knew my mom was there. I needed to get away from my stepmonster and father.

I asked my brother if he could come with me and he said yes. We got on our bikes and started our trip. We didn't get far that day. We were put in a car and taken home. That wasn't pretty, but it started the motion of moving back with Mom. By the time we finished that school year, Mom moved to Helena, Montana, and we were put on a plane and sent to live with her.

That was a beautiful day.

6:18 AM

I've been waking up in a very worried state.

I was thinking about past experiences that didn't work out.

I'm trying to figure out how to think about this. I am trying to stay present. It's hard to tell why I am laughing. My only goal is to stay present with my recovery.

10:36 AM

I don't remember the accident.

I don't even remember weeks before.

I don't even remember that Christmas.

I am working on trying to understand what happened; how could this happen to me? My life was perfect. My beautiful daughter had been off to college for the first year. I motorcycled every Sunday, which felt like church. I came from such a place of joy.

I heard stories about me getting up and trying to walk to the bathroom. That became quite a mess. I can see that these are stories, not memories. I do remember wanting to be home. I even woke up once, imagining being home then getting a little sad about how I remembered my home, thinking that it may not be what I think it is. My goal was always May 9 because the doctor told me that was when I could get out of my wheelchair and try to walk. Once I got out of the wheelchair, they said I could go home; I found out that the doctor had changed the date to May 18. I was not OK with that because I had always visualized being home for my birthday by May 12. The doctors and the nurses did not want me to go home until I walked. I worked hard to convince them, though I couldn't walk yet. They finally said yes, and the joy from my heart filled me for about another week until I could go home.

Another stage I remember was waking up in pain every day, but my goal was not to have to use diapers anymore. At first, it was just learning how to get to the toilet in the middle of the night, which I thought would be easy. I had to ask whoever was here at night to help. First, it was a nurse, then it was my mom, and by the time Grace came home from college, I had conquered this one...almost.

The other thing that I used to love was a hot bath every night. I remember that being a goal. At first, I knew I could get myself to sit in the tub, but I had to have somebody there who could pull me up. It seemed wild, but I was more than happy to take a bath even if somebody had to help me up and get out. I also remember the day I tried to do it independently, and it worked! Not daily, but a few times in a row.

DECEMBER 24, 2022
8:58 PM

Christmas Eve 2022

After a great day with my daughter and friends, I feel utterly exhausted. On my way home, I had a deep conversation with L. and G. about transition, patience, love, and healing. I now have a clear sense of purpose and direction for my writing.

DECEMBER 26, 2022
8:53 PM

Today, I came to understand the importance of achieving my goals to get back to where I once was. However, I have no desire to return to my past self. I find solace and growth in this journey of healing and recovery. While reminiscing about my previous activities, like going to the beach or enjoying the ocean, I long for those experiences once more. It's a struggle to regain all the things I used to love, but I must remind myself to be patient with this process. Recovery takes time, so I need to give myself grace and patience as I move toward a better future.

Texted my mom today. She asked what I'm doing for New Year's, and I said, "Plans are to wake up with a smile on my face and go to bed with a bigger one."

Today was the first day I gave myself the freedom to think about what it will take for me to fix my eye if I have to do that medically. This is all a reflection of how I felt post my wrist surgery. I felt more informed by the doctor.

" Everything is a gift of the universe –
even joy, anger, jealousy, frustration,
or separateness. Everything is
perfect either for our growth or
our enjoyment. "

– Ken Keyes Jr.

- More informed about the pros and cons.
- More informed about the pain and length of time.

I'm leaving the old Shannon Michelle behind. I'm leaving the old Shannon Michelle behind. I'm only showing up as the present, new Shannon Michelle.

DECEMBER 27, 2022
8:54 PM

Today's inspirational thought:

Side roads. You're where you're supposed to be at the moment you're supposed to be there. 😀 💜

DECEMBER 29, 2022
8:54 PM

Make the first report of what I'm expected I "can get back" mentally and physically.

• Full strength and usage of my body.
• Retaining my short-term memory.
• Feeling confident about getting back into design without feeling like it can overwhelm me.
• Not feeling so needy with my daughter.
• Being her place of strength and support again.
• My right eye working properly again.
• Finding my life partner.

DECEMBER 29, 2022
8:24 PM

Therapy questions today.

Dealing with worries about how others perceive me because of my lack of productivity and how to talk to them.

Considering the importance of discussing my accident with Grace to help her and understand its impact on her.

Concerned about not being able to remember recent therapy sessions due to short-term memory loss.

JANUARY 1, 2023
8:45 AM

Amos Lee, you have unknowingly been a crucial part of my recovery. Your music has helped countless people worldwide, including me. Today's song "Lightly" inspires me to pursue my goals with a light heart. The next track resonates even more deeply with its message of not facing challenges alone. Time passes swiftly, capturing the essence of life in the song "What's Been Going On."

8:51 PM

Feeling lost in the uncertainty of change, I used to think the New Year brought new opportunities, but now I'm not so sure. As I sit here in Los Angeles, I feel a strong difference between celebrating New Year's last year at my house with a very bright, pink Christmas tree in the window, all the people I love surrounding me that day. I cherished it, but what I realize is today I sit in my home alone on a day that I would spend with multiple people.

Every year life changes. So, I sit here at 9 p.m. and send hopes and dreams across to all the people I know in my heart. Tonight, being alone feels like a blessing.

JANUARY 2, 2023
8:53 PM

Moments of awakening. In a dream I woke up feeling like I was still in my current post-accident situation. I was at a store where I parked my car and went inside to buy something, then came out and realized that my car had been towed. I was about to call Grace to come pick me up, and then I woke up in bed, which made me realize that everything that I had just experienced was in a dream. Holy shit, that's new!
After such a trauma...you build back what you want to build back.
Not just because it was in your life before.

JANUARY 5, 2023
8:57 PM

I woke up in the middle of the night, which doesn't happen very often. I remembered being at a doctor's appointment. Grace was holding my

> **Be crumbled. So wild flowers will come up where you are. You have been stony for too many years. Try something different. Surrender.**
>
> — Rumi

hand, rubbing my fingers for quite some time. She kept looking at my hand and not letting it go. Then after a few minutes of doing that, Grace shared a memory about my hand being so swollen and yellow right after my accident. Grace said, "It's so good to see your hands the way they used to be, Mom." That was the first time she had a strong flashback to the moments at the hospital, not knowing if I was going to live or die. It felt good to have her share that with me.

JANUARY 7, 2023
8:52 PM
Freedom, strength, and understanding what I've been given from this life. Seeing, feeling, and knowing the freedom that has come as a gift from this accident.

JANUARY 14, 2023
3:42 PM
Grace left to go back to college. Today marked a significant moment as I finally found the ability to feel happiness instead of sadness when she left the house. It was a refreshing change from the usual feelings of loneliness and fear. This new day brought a sense of liberation and hope for what lies ahead. I woke up this morning, feeling like I did before my last surgery.

Another moment for me today was when I was lying on the table at cranial therapy with Teralis, who has been a godsend to my recovery. He was doing more cranial work, and I lay on the table and kept thinking about forgiveness, letting go, and freedom. The endless cycle of releasing and letting go kept replaying in my thoughts. Eventually, I understood that they were synonymous in the idea I was attempting to distinguish. It dawned on me that true liberation comes from setting things free.

JANUARY 16, 2023
9:34AM
As I relax after dinner tonight, I realize the importance of patience, but when I look down at my watch and I feel like it's time to go to bed and it's only 6 o'clock, it makes this moment feel like forever.

I feel like nobody has any idea of what it's like to lose what seems like everything—including my life—but my recovery from the brain trauma and the body surgeries were significant, and nobody understands.

I think I have so many people in my life who love me and support me through this process but don't quite understand the trauma of losing complete memory and short-term memory for months. They believe that it all will comes back to me, but it doesn't. It wasn't until I faced the challenges head-on that I began to see the gaps in my capabilities. This realization marks a turning point, prompting a shift in how I approach learning and memory retention.

I keep hearing my friends tell me that I already said that or "don't you remember, blah blah blah, being at the hospital visiting you." I could go on for weeks or months with how many versions of that I have heard, and people are just trying to support me when they say that, but at some points it feels overwhelming.

Depressing.

In the first seven months after coming home, I avoided conversations that could frighten or limit me due to my brain injury. Even asking for help from a friend was a big step forward for me.

Learning to communicate my needs was a pivotal moment in my recovery process. I realized that vulnerability is not a weakness, but rather a bridge to deeper connections and understanding with those around me. Each small victory felt monumental, slowly piecing together my sense of self that the injuries seemed to have scattered.

What the fuck, that's progress!

JANUARY 17, 2023
3:08 PM
Questions for today's therapy session.
Expectations of friends.

I learned that I didn't depend on them enough before the accident, but now I feel like they don't check in or do as much as they did before. I know I'm limited, but I'm still here.
Dating again?
Regular amount of time to expect my daughter to check in?

Discussing today in session from therapist: Keeping an accounting of my progress and future expected growth every three months would allow me to see in real terms the progress of my recovery.

The other purpose of this is to determine when I need to create rituals/work-arounds so I can enjoy a higher level of functionality (i.e., feel more solid). For example: Having a "go-to" place with lists and images that remind me of things I want to recall and can't necessarily do so anymore with just my memory.

Daily walking again.
No more headaches.

HOMEWORK:
Understand how I'm perceived post-accident and why some friends seemingly treat me differently.

Less headache pain.

Make the first report of what I'm expect I "can get back" mentally and physically.

Right eye recovery.

FEBRUARY 3, 2023
8:15 AM
For the last five days I awoke with no head pain or headache. This is the first time since the last surgery that I have felt good for this long.

FEBRUARY 6, 2023
8:41 AM

I woke up this morning with a spiritual "hello" from my grandmother, Rose. I was back in my childhood memories of sitting in her dining room. I had an amazing dream where I talked to my client D. about the layout of her master closet. It was the first time I dreamed about work. This brought me such joy to wake up from a clear and vivid dream.

My reactions, understanding, and responses made them see the person they once knew in a whole new light. It was ironic yet powerful to share that this was a rebirth—a new, more advanced version of myself emerging.

More spiritual.
More open.
Freedom.

Of my spiritual growth, I know that I am not afraid of death any longer. There was a day death came very close, and I was in between earth and heaven being held so beautifully by Bill Langford. I can see it, and it looks like the place I would much rather be.

I needed a reassuring presence in our shared space, guiding me through moments of uncertainty until I found safety and clarity.

Wow, those memories of my existence in the center of the universe will never leave me.

On February 6, I was happy, happy, happy!

I woke up this morning to myself accepting, understanding, loving, committing, and joyful of my rebirth.
In my morning meditation, I kept repeating (hearing) "Take care of your mind, body, heart, and soul."

" The point of power is always in the present moment. "

– Louise L. Hay

FEBRUARY 27, 2023
4:54 PM
I know I need to give myself the freedom and space to just sit and be sad, but I don't know if I remembered how to do that before all this happened. I kept things moving; I kept things busy; I kept things far away from this loneliness, the sadness before my accident. I never let sadness come in like this. I need a way to deal with being alone again.

If you need to be sad...
Be sad.
Find the time and space to cry.

MARCH 3, 2023
6:37 PM
After having full anesthesia for my last surgery, it set me back in ways that I could never imagine and that the doctors never thought that something like that could have. It was a shit show, and it scared the crap out of me because I knew that I had more surgeries to go through. I could barely sit up or function, body- or brain-wise. It was so bad that my daughter had to take me to the emergency room two days after my last surgery. It took over a week to get back into my body, and I lost around six months of progress with my brain recovery.

Questions for neurologist and psychiatrist:
After the last surgery on November 22, I had a horrible reaction to the anesthesia. I severely regressed both cognitively and physically to the point where I had to go to the emergency room. I was told before that surgery that going under anesthesia would not be a problem. What do you suggest I do, moving forward when I need anesthesia for either local or general? Is one preferred over the other? Will the choice of local with light sedation have the same impact, since it is a mind-altering medication?

Does time help alleviate the symptoms of regression? Is there any data on others with a severe traumatic brain injury having a similar experience under anesthesia?

Can you give me less anesthesia? Maybe I had too much?
Healing does not have a time limit.

MARCH 5, 2023
11:16 AM
Birds are an important part of my recovery. I know that I was rebirthed through this process. I became a phoenix to rebuild and rebirth myself up in the sky.

In the sky, I was looking up and then looking down, and to be able to come back down to earth, I needed a spiritual death of Shannon Michelle 1.0.
As I woke up and started re-creating my brain, birds and butterflies brought joy to my daily recovery. They still do. I look out my bedroom window at the first bird feeder we hung a few months ago, and there's a collection of birds that come and go.

Balancing strength, understanding, kindness, and love is Shannon 2.0
Shannon 2.0 is an unstoppable, positive energy.

Shannon 2.0 no longer lives in fear or hesitation like Shannon 1.0 sometimes did.

MARCH 12, 2023
8:50 PM
Today was the first day I woke up feeling like one million bucks, pre-medication.

I set up my dining table in such joy that I thought I didn't even need to pray for myself today, and then I was going to pray for Grace. I started saying a little prayer for her and realized that she's covered as well.

We're both covered. We're all covered, and the only reason why we wake up needing to say prayers is for some power or to control how things will work out.
Isn't that the funniest thing: believing that our efforts alone determine our outcomes when, in reality, we are part of a greater plan?

" I have the ability to direct my own thoughts. "

– Jerry Hicks

Also, on a miraculous and beautiful note, this is coming from a place of want, not need. For so many months, I would wake up in the morning trying to achieve more, making sure that I didn't lose something. Now I wake up enjoying whatever comes to me and not trying to overcome my accident, not trying to overcome my brain loss, not trying to overcome what happened, but trying to be present in each and every moment. This way of being comes from not being fearful of loss, but understanding the gain and beauty of life.

For today, live moment-by-moment.
In doing so, you will be fearless.

Second big, big, big lesson: I know that I have many earth angels, but today I realized the ones who are in my heart, and they have been such a huge part of my recovery. I never really thought of earth angels in these terms. I have two who are so different from each other.

Dana is my earth angel of love, kindness, security. She is soft, beautiful, and generous.

Jessica is my earth, angel of strength, forgiveness, sorrow, and abundance. She is the one who shows me less patience, which reminds me of my strength.

MARCH 13, 2023
2:04 PM
I just got another sign. I was walking and saw my neighbor, Tina, who has helped me over the last six months. Whenever I reach out, she is there with her arms open. I shared with her that I live guided by my feelings, and that's how I live each day. Patience is my strongest virtue.

MARCH 14, 2023
8:00 AM
Today all I could think about was "just show up." This is a new process for me. As Shannon 1.0, I worried too much about how I looked or how other things showed up.

Let go of worries about appearances or assumptions. Embrace being present without judgment. How we show up is what we receive.

For today, "just show up" for yourself. Take a moment to look in the mirror and repeat: "I am full of beauty, strength, and brilliance, no matter how I dress or look!

MARCH 16, 2023
7:00 PM
I just read my fortune cookie: "Your courage will reward you."

Today was difficult. I woke up with a terrible headache, and it did not go away all day long. I haven't had my cranial therapy today, which I know brings a certain amount of help and relief, but this was not that day. But that's OK, too. We learn and we learn and we learn that doesn't always change, but that doesn't mean that bad days still don't happen.

Here's the good news, yesterday was the second time in the past year that I have been able to drive myself to one of my medical appointments at Kaiser.

How we teach ourselves to want something, but not need something in this moment again: I went to bed the night before, wanting to be able to drive myself but also expecting to wake up in a position where I didn't feel safe or have enough energy to drive myself. But I did wake up strong. I woke up clear. I woke up feeling very capable, and that was a win-win.

MARCH 19, 2023
4:40 AM
Sunday morning. Woke up in this morning's dream where I had been sitting on the toilet taking a shit and was wiping the remnants off my ass. I was wiping away my pain and getting better and better and better, but it took a long time to clean up the shit. It was such a realistic dream that, when I woke up, I realized I was in my bedroom and it was not really happening as I was wiping my ass in the dream. And I didn't have to wake up to take a shit, which I couldn't understand.

It makes me believe that, in my dream/spirit life, I was having a hard time getting the final pieces of shit off my ass.

There has been so much crap in my body and my brain over this past year since my motorcycle accident. I feel like each day I am slowly getting more and more crap off my body and mind. And I think this morning's dream was that. I was very close, but not completely done with getting all the shit off my ass...maybe?

I really want to remember the gifts I've given myself in this Shannon 2.0 process.

Another thing that I have been learning about myself, is "just to show up and be present" and "not worry about how you look or what you say, but just be present."

MARCH 20, 2023
3:00 PM
Monday. How does that feel?
Today feels powerful at some moments and more overwhelming than others. I was just in my kitchen taking a few things down off my pin board that didn't need to be there anymore, giving myself room to grow and change.

Change what I see.
Change what I do.

I recently rediscovered a small piece of artwork I had created. While I don't recall exactly when I painted it, I realized today that it depicts me in different stages of my life. In the painting, I'm in an ocean setting, relaxing and also sitting on the sand in front of a house. At the time I didn't recognize it, but now I see that it represents my past and present selves. This realization highlighted the magical way our subconscious and conscious minds support each other.

MARCH 31, 2023
1:39 PM
Stop judging people!
Trust in others' sharing, without the need for a response or full understanding. Simply trust and let them reveal their true intentions. Whether positive or negative, it ultimately doesn't matter.

1:48 PM
I am beautiful! Again, don't make it a comparison. Stop comparing yourself to others to make yourself feel better.

It used to work for me, but it doesn't any longer. Embrace the honesty and truth in acknowledging your unique beauty.

The only place where comparing is valuable is when you're shopping.

APRIL 1, 2023
3:00 PM
Can you just watch?
Stay silent and learn?

9:41PM
Simple question:
Have your moments of hardships:
Hurt you?
Taught you?
Or built you?
They have built me.

Deeper, Lighter, Stronger, Freer!
Ying and yang! That statement I never truly believed or understood until tonight.
Soulfully.
Slow and steady wins the race. That's what I feel (and know).

APRIL 2, 2023
3:54 PM
Grateful for the clarity of connecting with the good and the bad. Not trying to avoid just the bad.

Grateful for my daughter, Grace.
Kindness.
Thoughtfulness.
Open and loving heart.
Balanced in this life on all levels.

APRIL 10, 2023
9:34 PM
I'm experiencing the gift of Shannon Michelle 2.0. The new me has a presence that embraces listening without judgment or the need to be right. In this space, understanding flows effortlessly, allowing for meaningful connections and insights to emerge naturally.

There is no need to be right.
Just listen.

APRIL 17, 2023
5:05 AM
I don't live in the past anymore, and I don't live in a wishful future. I love the present, in this moment every day, every minute.

This is permission to dream now.
Let's get busy living for today.
Start with gratitude and appreciation.

I'm also learning about this fearful part of my past existence, or if I believe something and know something, it would scare me, and I would talk myself out of it. But from Shannon 2.0, I am not going to get fearful of my spirit messages because these are not dreams, they are actually messages from my spirit guides.

> **When I received the phone call with my biopsy results, my doctor carefully told me I had breast cancer. To my surprise, I started laughing.**
>
> – Shannon Michelle

APRIL 22, 2023
3:26 PM
Today was a tough day. Overall, it was fine, but there were multiple times when I felt sad and alone. It's hard to have those feelings and not get depressed, but at the same time, they're just feelings for today, and I need to put them to rest and start over tomorrow.

It's OK to have a bad day. I have to keep reminding myself that in life in general, even without the trauma, every day has some good and bad. So, today is one of those days.

Sadness, hard days, weakness...
We all look at them no matter what we believe. Sometimes we think that if we do enough of the right things or we make enough right choices, we can leave behind sadness or pain, but it's really not how it all works, no matter what we all feel.

2:50 AM
I woke up in fear and sadness. Just had to remind myself that this happens, too.

APRIL 24, 2023
4:48 AM
Achieving happiness lies in striking a balance between the good and the bad. Embrace both parts equally: they are essential to our journey.

APRIL 28, 2023
8:46 PM
In a moment of reflection, I realized I don't need to doubt myself. I choose to be here: strong, supported, and loving myself. Despite moments of doubt and confusion, when we connect with our heart and soul, we find peace. Let's embrace self-love every day.

APRIL 30, 2023
4:13 PM
I am so sad today. Yesterday was all right. Insanely busy day.

I have breast cancer.

I also got my paperwork from Kaiser to get to the UCLA eye surgery, so that's moving ahead. Honestly, I don't even know how to feel about all this, I am very overwhelmed. I feel in my heart that I'm going to be OK, but I'm breathless.

Today, I'm just feeling really tired, so strong yet tired. I want to go away, but obviously that's not going to happen until I do a little bit more work on this body of mine.

MAY 5, 2023
5:41 PM

Happy Cinco de Mayo! Today was a powerful day. I finally had my eye surgery at UCLA and was so excited for this day. I wasn't thinking about or realizing how much pain it would be. I think I was just focusing on the end result. With such trauma I've experienced, what I have been trying to teach myself is how much progress I have made.

Big picture.
Big picture.
Big picture.

MAY 7, 2023
12:03 PM

Happy Sunday!

Transforming the Innerliving office into a serene writing and art retreat has been my key focus. Every corner of my home and guest house is now a sanctuary filled with joy, reflecting my journey toward healing and self-care.

Create a beautiful space for yourself.
It can be a corner of a room or a small space you can claim as yours.
Set your intentions for your haven.
Let it be a sanctuary for rest, creativity, and healing.

MAY 16, 2023
7:48 AM
Grateful, grateful, grateful.
Sometimes you have these moments in life, these disturbing and uncomfortable feelings, and then moments later you feel enlightened.

It can be hard to accept something that feels painful. But many times, it turns into enlightenment and a gift. I was on the phone with my friend today, and she was expressing how often sharing something can be harmful for somebody else and it's best to ask yourself that question before saying anything. She was quoting a concept out of a book about sobriety.

In Shannon Michelle 2.0, authenticity reigns. When our hearts and souls speak the truth, we embrace it openly and fearlessly. No need for cover-ups—just genuine expression.

Again, hiding our truth to keep others safe is not the right decision. People grow, including us, from the good and the bad.

Please don't let your trauma hide your authentic self.

This life is a continuous cycle of growth, where our actions impact others. We struggle with what to share and what not to share. It's important to remember that we all have different perspectives based on our experiences and needs.

12:11 PM
Focus on myself. OK, I love you, yeah.
What we intend we get, so we have to intend greatly.

MAY 17, 2023
2:19 AM

P, P, P.
Motherfucker, I haven't done that in a while. I find it embarrassing and

frustrating that I went to the bathroom while sleeping last night. It has been a long time since I've done a PBP in my bed. Sometimes, things happen, and they make no sense. But on the other hand, it is just a reminder that I am still in recovery. It's also a reminder that things are broken and need to be repaired, even on a day I would never have thought that would happen.

Sometimes, we need reminders. And I'm unsure if it's a reminder that silly things still happen on this journey of patience, patience, patience, baby steps.

What do I need as a reminder? It has been one year and a half since my accident. Sometimes, we need to be reminded that the road is long. The road is hard, and the road is not over.

How long does it take, and how long has it taken to make such a childlike boo-boo accidentally? I've been home from the hospital for one year. The biggest reminder is that when we think we're on the other end of doing something or being a certain way, we are sometimes reminded that we're not. Crazy motherfucker, this body!

I just realized that I was so relaxed, comfortable, and confident that I ended up peeing in bed without worrying about the moment when I briefly woke up to go to the bathroom. My body was so exhausted and relaxed at the same time, and I could do that with such comfort.

9:05 PM
If the list couldn't get any bigger...
I got a text from my brother that my dad died.
Peace. Patience. Joy.

MAY 25, 2023
4:16 PM
Some days, those of us with massive injuries wake up feeling so needy and so unimportant that it hurts us mentally and physically. This accident and this very long recovery have given me a gift to see myself

on all sides. I was not a person, in my previous life as successful, who saw the negative side of myself or my history. I truly believed that the more I distanced myself from my traumas or didn't share them, the farther away they would be from me, and that would make my life better. Denying that trauma would make my life different from my two parents, and that was a big goal.

Because of my awful childhood, I just taught myself how to be the opposite of what I was raised by. And, as much success that brought me, it also brought the limitations I see now. It taught me not to trust men. I believed that if I were smart enough, I would succeed.

We don't always realize that we must be open to both sides: the good and the bad, the successful and the needy, the love and hate, the strong and the weak. Life is two-sided; if we can't understand and learn from each side, we don't learn balance.

When I woke up from my accident, I sat in all levels of fear. Fear of what was taken. Fear of what I had lost. Fear of what I could regain. That person who had woken up from the accident was not the same person whose body was found unconscious on the Pacific Coast Highway. Fear is what takes everything from us emotionally. It is wet, leaves us in the dark, and doesn't allow us to see the light.

I realized that I need to wake up every day and stay present. I need to stay in the moment of that minute, that breath, that feeling.

Living fully in the present moment is our greatest strength.

By the way, this morning when I woke up, I felt joy, I felt excitement. I felt hopeful. That's not every day, but it is today.

TRAUMATIC BRAIN INJURY RECOVERY

A month ago, my psychiatrist instructed me to take a cognitive test, so they could help guide my recovery and understand my limitations. I asked what I could do daily to help my brain recover, and this test was the next step. That psychiatrist called me yesterday and said the test results were in and that she was impressed at my recovery, considering my accident and my brain trauma.

I want to know how to improve, grow, learn, and retain. That's all I was asking, but I still surprise people with my recovery so far. They almost talk to me like I shouldn't be alive or conscious.

We are surrounded by angels, and together, we're doing a lot more work.

MAY 26, 2023
11:23 AM

Today, I felt inspired to reflect on personal stories worth sharing. I was on the phone with a brain psychologist, sharing my history and explaining how I understand my progress. The moment I woke up, my daughter, Grace, was about to leave to go back to college. All I wished for was a walk with her and our dog before she left. I wanted to know that I could do it again once she was gone.

Overcoming intense fear held me back from simple tasks like walking my dog during my recovery journey. But I managed to conquer that level of fear and find my way out.

My daughter became the mother figure, bringing me out of fear of everything. I would relive every moment as if it were the first time. Fear of walking my dog: LOL, it just seems ironic. It seems funny to know this was a fear. But we all need these moments to see our progress and understand where we've come from and where we want to go.

Again, I am a miracle.
The other thing I realize as I speak into my phone to write this journal is that I don't remember everything I say. I don't know everything I have talked into my phone while writing this book, and I look forward to reading you, understanding you, and remembering our history together. The other decisive moment I was given today was when my brain therapist said, "Be here now."

" Gratitude makes sense of our past, brings peace for today, and creates a vision for tomorrow. "

– Melody Beattie

These are the questions we ask ourselves in recovery:
How much pain does your body feel today?
How much resistance and emptiness does the brain feel?
What can I do today?
What can I do right now to get myself out of bed?

MAY 31, 2023
5:18 PM
Breast doctor, Kaiser Permanente: surgery tomorrow, June 1.

Today I feel...Tired... overwhelmed... depressed.
Excited... overwhelmed... hopeful
You could call this a 50-50 day!

Power and insight are so clear at this moment. By the end of the session, my therapist who suffered from TBI as well, said, "You should write a book." I did need to hear that again. With so many road bumps, it's easy to get distracted by all the mess, by all I forget, by how I feel (all the difficulties).

9:34 PM
Surgery tomorrow: it's going to go easily, and it's not going to affect my brain capacity-building.
 Good night.

JUNE 1, 2023
9:35 AM
Breast cancer removal day.

One of the nurses suggested that I read, You Are the Placebo: Making Your Mind. She was such a support for me, helping me make decisions pre-surgery.

Recognition is at the heart of being. Gertrude Stein said, "I am, because my little dog knows me." Is there a difference between being and being seen?

You may need help seeing exactly where you're headed. In moments like these, you are forced to let go of control.

JUNE 4, 2023
7:28 PM
We are not here to fix things. We are here to experience, and that only happens by staying present (not trying to learn to fix shit). This is difficult but most important.

Headaches are painful. That's it. We don't have to make them go away, but don't make them a reason not to be happy. They fucking suck.
Let's make that clear.

7:46 PM
I am so tired today, but I did nothing at all.
Tired, tired, tired.

JUNE 9, 2023
6:27 PM
Post-trauma, post-beautiful life days can feel very confusing. Why do I remember one thing and not another?

Explaining who I am now may be confusing. Some still see me as I once was, assuming less trauma occurred and underestimating the impact of my TBI. Despite these challenges, I embrace my new identity as a "rebuilt" or "rebirth" of my soul.

I just heard inner calm is your most valuable asset. Peace and acceptance are my most valuable assets.

JUNE 12, 2023
6:51 PM
Today fucking sucked. I had to do my first Social Security doctor appointment. Like I have already been through enough of these conversations. It's hard when your brain repeats and you keep getting reminded of your struggles and your hard recovery moments. Always staying hopeful is not happening today.

JUNE 16, 2023
1:18 PM
I sat on the toilet, and all I could think about was guarding my breasts from cancer. I had a breast lift and implants because my appearance was so important to me.
Sometimes we are too vain. I had never thought of this recovery, including breast cancer from this position. I always keep the excuse that I got my boobs fixed because of my breast-feeding. They were always big, but I just wanted my nipples not to look down and I wanted them to look out and be perky.

Your ego can get very messy very quickly if you let it. Don't let your ego spiral out of control. Stop feeding into the need for validation and find peace in simply being.

JUNE 20, 2023
9:00 AM
When I woke up this morning, I had this realization that I didn't know the correct answer to my breast situation. Cancer means I haven't been given the right answer yet. The minute I do, I will know it's the best choice for these next steps.

Sometimes the best thing to do is nothing.
Take time to rest.
Be present.
Trust that the solution will come at the right time.

JUNE 25, 2023
3:45 AM
Through our discussion on death, I've come to realize that people often operate from a mindset of gain or loss. Many individuals distance themselves from those who make them feel inferior. It's crazy how we constantly compare ourselves and base our connections on what we stand to gain or lose.

In the end, people's choices are guided by what they believe will benefit them in the long term, whether it seems positive or negative at first glance. Again, being gracious, being inviting, being thoughtful is for the better in the long run.

#Truth #Patience #Discovery

The other brilliant news is that I went to bed a little after 9:00 PM and didn't wake up until 6:15 AM. I didn't wake up to go to the bathroom in the middle of the night or worry about anything for any reason. I slept through the night.

JUNE 25, 2023
6:56 AM
Good morning. I have this period of time (hard week) when I realize my recovery is less than I really understand. My recovery, mostly my primary brain recovery and slightly in my body recovery, is at a much slower pace.

Did that mean I'm supposed to understand how much brain function I regain? Do I have to understand what short-term memory I have forgotten and will not get back? I get very confused sometimes and feel depressed.

Sadness.

Do others feel this way with such a major recovery?
Do we just continue to teach ourselves to be new versions of ourselves, no matter what?

The hardest thing for me this week was going to a mandatory doctor's appointment, so I can keep getting my Social Security benefits.

Although it is important for me to receive financial assistance, it was difficult for me to accept that I need this much care.

It is not giving up, it is accepting.

" Comparing is the opposite of recovery. Just sit still. Just be patient. Just be grateful. "

– Shannon Michelle

Unveiling the truth: Being needy doesn't equate to strength or intelligence. Formerly a caretaker, I now strive to embrace a brighter perspective amid a tragic reality. Even though this feels very tragic, I have to learn a new way of existing in a positive light.

How do I see myself in a beautiful way?
How is so much neediness a beautiful thing?
How do I not get depressed when so much has been taken from me?

Yesterday, my daughter took me into a little shop after we left the doctor's appointment and bought me a gift. Her kindness resonates. She said her kindness in doing that for me was something I used to do for her when she was little. Her thoughtful gesture reminded me that kindness is timeless and still a part of my identity.

I understand loss now. It is a feeling that I cannot fully explain or teach. We all experience some level of loss and tragedy, but it affects each of us differently. The only way we can truly understand others is by seeing them as equals, regardless of where we come from.

It's important to just listen without trying to relate or understand and simply accept.

JUNE 28 2023
5:29 PM
Today was hard!
Fucked up date of my next breast cancer surgery. It's not July 3, it's July 19. Hard item to fuck up the dates on. It doesn't feel very good today.

It's OK and KIND
not to remember everything

JULY 4, 2023
1:01 PM
Impossible things happen every day.
That is a lesson worth living.
At least worth knowing.

JULY 14, 2023
8:24 AM
Good morning. I'm learning that I need to focus on what truly matters during my traumatic brain injury recovery. I need to prioritize what's important to me. Where do I invest my time and energy? I need to release any unnecessary distractions that do not contribute to my progress.
I was lucky enough to spend the last two days beach camping. I still adore the beach, so I woke up this morning thinking my newest route is taking the bus to the beach when it's important. I can do that.

JULY 16, 2023
3:11 AM
I woke up, so scared and overwhelmed.
Breathe, Shannon, breathe.
Remember that you never have to feel normal again.
And yes, that is a gift.
A gift of freedom? I don't know.
Somethings I'm never going to know and that's OK.

JULY 18, 2023
7:21 AM
I don't know, I don't know, I don't know.
That is how I'm feeling.

JULY 23, 2023
6:02 AM
Sunday. Breast cancer, for me, is learning how to be different. How to feel different means visually seeing yourself differently; but, most importantly, everybody in every walk of life is different.

Don't try to build your strength off of how you visually look. It builds your strength of how you see yourself, not how you're seen; yesterday was a challenging day to look at myself in the mirror and see my tits, not just different sizes, but very awkward and uneven. Bumpy in different ways. That was very alarming. I was expecting my boobs to look small and saggy, but not so broken and bumpy.

I'm here for me in my life. Being able to prepare myself and visualize something has made it simpler to deal with trauma, but the reality is you don't even know what you're going to get. And that's going to be OK, too. It surely doesn't feel OK right now. It makes me so sad and overwhelmed.

I am a woman who brings perspective from the other end of things.

JULY 25, 2023
7:48 AM
Comparing is the opposite of recovery.
Just sit still.
Just be patient.
Just be grateful.

JULY 28, 2023
11:11 AM
I am made of stardust and grace.
There is more than one way to open a path.
I am going down in this second life.

JULY 30, 2023
3:03 PM
To feel safe.
To be seen.
To be loved.

Strength from my traumatic brain injury. Learning how to deal with remembering everything, especially short-term memory loss. I'm learning to be more kind with myself when I don't remember so much.
It's not important to remember what you said or what you've done, but who you are.

What am I grateful for:
My strength in recovery.
My kindness to myself and others, even when I've been scared.
My breast cancer for teaching me that I still need to slow down in my recovery.

Remember that we are not done yet, and that is OK.
Patience, patience, patience.

5:23 PM
Patience, fucking patience, fucking patience!
Or is it patients fucking patience fucking patience?
Or is it really...

Patience, fucking patience, fucking patience!

Broken is beautiful.
To be able to see yourself in many, many, many different parts is gorgeous.

Perfection sucks. Broken is real.

AUGUST 10, 2023
9:01 PM
Exhausted.

I'm super grateful that I have to do radiation and not chemo. That brought me joy and relief as well as such sorrow at the same time. Then anger and fear filled my heart. This road wiped me out emotionally.
Tears of joy?

Either way, it doesn't matter because I am exhausted, and the bottom line is this road will be much softer than the chemo road.
And at the end of this celebratory day, I only want to sleep and play a little solitaire.

AUGUST 22, 2023
7:38 AM
Today fucking sucks.
Overwhelmed, overwhelmed, overwhelmed.
Sad. Sad. Sad.
Motherfucker.

> **And the light will enter.**
> **Always does.**
>
> – Kamal Ravikant

I'm supposed to have my UCLA follow-up surgeon appointment today, but it didn't work out. Grace took off work this morning to take me, but when we got there, they said they couldn't have me until Kaiser approved that appointment. It's tough to be so excited about answers, progress, or possibilities and not have any of that happen.

AUGUST 23, 2023
5:45 AM
Insecurity is such a powerful weapon.
It will let you forget who you truly are.
Insecurity teaches you how not to believe in yourself. You know who you are.

Sometimes you have to learn to live your life relying on your heart and soul more than you do your eyes. Insight is deeper than seeing.

SEPTEMBER 11, 2023
7:53 AM
Today was a tough day, because sometimes you realize your progress but then run into a few walls and roadblocks. It makes you question your own self-knowledge.

Strength in recovery does not mean completion. This is life.

SEPTEMBER 13, 2023
7:50 AM
Today's TBI gift was realizing that I could be "strong and silent" simultaneously. That was a gift I had before my accident, but when you come out of such a chaotic, life-changing, brain-changing experience, there is a need to ask three million questions a day: some to reboot, some to relearn, and some to build strength and know who you are and what you have become.

SEPTEMBER 17, 2023
11:14 AM
"Just be" is big and beautiful.
I needed to break to truly open!

SEPTEMBER 18, 2023
6:14 PM
Days keep terrorizing into the night.

SEPTEMBER 19, 2023
1:19 PM
It's a good thing to ask yourself anytime you feel sad or fearful, or you're trying to make changes:

SEPTEMBER 20, 2023
7:43 PM
Last day of radiation:
Grateful
Loved
Balanced
Surrounded by love.

SEPTEMBER 22, 2023
2:47 PM
New stepping stones with friends?
Creating new stepping stones in my life.
I don't know how. 😅

SEPTEMBER 29, 2023
8:52 PM
I guess the bigger question is...
Why are we on this road?

No matter how you got to this page, we are ALL together. I'm sure we all have unique and mind-blowing stories. But honestly, we were all in the same place.

OCTOBER 4, 2023
8:56 PM
I am whole.
I am pure love.
I am kindness.

I am pure life.
I am scared.
I am lonely.
I am all sides of light and dark—happy and sad.

Truly, my biggest gifts are "knowing but not knowing" reboots. It's like knowing most all spiritual insight, but not truly knowing the words that match it. I'm here to share my story with you, and I am very hopeful that you will receive it somehow.

Post traumatic brain injury may leave a person very scared, very unknown, and very fearful. To have to "relearn" everything again is frightening.

At 53, I learned how to read again, use a computer again, use the telephone again, learn verbiage and meanings again. It's mind-blowing. We don't know how much we have to lose until we lose it all.

I know that this universe is one big, full, meaningful circle of love. We are all one.

You need to hear this.
Everything is possible.

OCTOBER 16, 2023
11:11 AM
I get sad.
I get scared.
I get lonely.

Then, I remember that these days just get fewer and fewer, and it reminds me of my resilience and strength.

OCTOBER 22, 2023
8:56 PM
There's a moment when you realize, in your life, the things that excite you and that make you breathless may all be so similar. But even more

> **Always remember you are braver than you believe, stronger than you seem, smarter than you think and twice as beautiful as you'd ever imagined. Yesterday I was clever, so I wanted to change the world. Today I am wise, so I am changing myself.**
>
> – Rumi

enlightening is that when something like the freedom and breathlessness of riding a motorcycle can turn into the breathlessness when you get to learn how to play solitaire—and win!

Is that crazy talk?
Is that feeling enlightened?
Or is that just feeling balanced?
Well, I just did win!

What you realize is that whatever leaves you breathless and makes you feel like a winner is all the same.

9:34 PM
Where do you find joy?
So, don't stand in your own way.
Finish your fucking book, Shannon.
This is your next chapter in life...

Just keep pursuing where are you find joy in each moment, and the rest will find its way.

OCTOBER 24, 2023
11:44 AM
"Hey there, dial up the beauty! I understand and support your efforts. Shannon, I love you! Let's focus on what really matters. Don't worry about my taxes: let's commit to bigger things that are essential. It's time to tackle the chaos in our lives and get things done efficiently. Let's stop procrastinating and handle the priorities. No more excuses; it's time for action!"

OCTOBER 29, 2023
8:37 PM
Another super proud day of my recovery. I did a gentle yoga class.

NOVEMBER 1, 2023
4:24 PM

This makes me laugh: I can live through a motorcycle accident and breast cancer, but I can't deal with only four hours of sleep!

I'm learning how to take the bus to Kaiser. I walked many blocks and sat down for 10 minutes, and the bus passed me right by. Even though it was late, I just kept going.

And now I sit here in the open space to be seen and wait for the next bus. Patience, patience, patience.

As I sit here and wait for the next bus, I'll look across the way and see people driving and the energy and lack of enjoyment. I see their faces; it reminds me how we all struggle differently.

4:34 PM

How is it so exhausting to learn how to be patient? Patience is a strong goal, and I often achieve it, but sometimes it just feels very exhausting to be patient.

NOVEMBER 2, 2023
8:22 PM

Allow yourself to just cruise thought life, not drive.

Epiphany: A big gift to yourself is forgiveness. No, that's not right. I don't have to forgive myself. I need to just stay present, and that will be a perfect state. It's also OK not to remember what you did or said; remembering present moments is not necessary in building your strength.

NOVEMBER 5, 2023
7:07 AM

Stay present, and it will work itself out.

Roads are long and bumpy, but they are always leading us to the right place.

NOVEMBER 12, 2023
11:05 PM
Tell me your story.
Personal transformation and social transformation happen at the same time. Growth is equal to transformation.

NOVEMBER 14, 2023
4:47 PM
Top five repairs and recoveries for brain trauma.

TBI repairs 101
Sleep: In sleep our brain heals.
Fear: How to move safely through the fear of total loss and abandonment.
Loss: How to move from feeling like there's a huge loss to magical miracle.

Connecting with others: Understand that you were placed in the world post brain trauma. What does this feel like?

Help: Daily rituals help rebuild this brain. Daily ways to help your friends and family truly connect to you again.

NOVEMBER 25, 2023
7:15 PM
I was an avoidant personality before my motorcycle accident.

DECEMBER 2, 2023
4:54 AM
Boom. I woke up this morning with all kinds of memories. But it started with a fearful memory about an individual who was trying to sue me after my accident. People don't balance out the yin and yang. The black and the white. The positive with the negative. Everything has more than one side. Now I understand how humans only take things from their own perspective without looking at the whole situation. That is very one-sided. We learn that how we show up, react, and think has everything to do with who we are, and that affects others.

DECEMBER 4, 2023
7:15 AM
Monday. Sometimes I just have to remember I belong to me.
That isn't always easy.

It's the difference of coming up with I belong to me, but we are all one in this universe. So truly when I feel alone, I am never alone.
We are all one.

7:52 AM
Adaptability is the key.
But more importantly, we are the key to our joy and not others' opinions of us.

How do we work that out? We are one, but we have to take care of ourselves first.

Oh, we are all one. So, take care of yourself no matter what. Got it.

8:42 AM
People in general do look for a version or an excuse as to why something bad happens or why somebody treats you a certain way. But the bottom line is you get what you get, and you don't get upset because it's all about you. It's all about us; there is no blame needed.

Hating a person does not help you grow.

Hating a situation does not get you enlightened.

So, please stop finding excuses, blame, or feeling hatred in your life.

DECEMBER 6, 2023
9:48 AM
Find comfort in communities that reflect your values and safety in being part of a group like you.

"
It's not important to remember
what you said or what you've
done, but who you are.

"

— Shannon Michelle

Embrace growth by stepping out of your comfort zone and engaging with diverse perspectives.

There is a power in surrounding yourself with both like-minded individuals and those who are different.
Strength is built through this balance of similarities and differences.
Our perceptions are shaped by our experiences and knowledge.
Increasing your experiences will increase your knowledge.

2:17 PM
TBIs definitely come from all walks of life: something as simple as falling and hitting your head at any age to a severe motorcycle accident to a stroke and age disabilities.

We all need help.

Brain usage versus brain capability: does that matter?

Discovering the impact of my presence was a revelation. Initially, I believed it stemmed from gratitude for not experiencing my struggles. Now, I understand that my journey through adversity has inspired others to seek my perspective and guidance on overcoming challenges.

I'm enlightening.
I'm inspiring.
I am insightful.
I am helpful.
I'm a barometer for others, as well as myself.

DECEMBER 9, 2023
5:02 PM
Every experience, whether tragic or traumatic, is a lesson in disguise. Take a moment to pause and listen, as each challenge brings valuable insights on our journey through life.

> " To be able to see yourself in many, many, many different parts is gorgeous. Perfection sucks. Broken is real.

— Shannon Michelle

What are some challenges in your life that turn out to be blessings?
1.
2.
3.

Don't question.
Just pause.

Understand that what we receive is a reflection of our ability to give and take. It's important to embrace both the positive and negative aspects of life.

6:13 PM
Shit. I tried to do too much today, I guess.
It's funny how you forget how pain feels when you push through so much of it and it's been a while.
It really hurts.
My body talked, and I needed to listen.
My lesson is to not do so much yet.

DECEMBER 10, 2023
10:23 AM
How do we ever know?
How do we ever know what street to walk down?
How do we know what question to ask?
How do we know if we could've made it differently?
How do we ever know we've made the right choices?
How do we ever know if the sorrow will become lighter?
Honestly, will I ever know?
Will I ever understand?
I think that's what scares me the most some days.

I know if I repeat over and over and over and over again "stay present, stay present, stay present," it grounds me and lowers my stress.

DECEMBER 13, 2023
8:04 AM
Love sometimes = fear

Oh, that's OK, too. When I'm asked to think and focus on one word, "love" is what came to me. Then "fear," and it made me realize that they were sometimes equal to each other in my mind.

I will work on separating the two.
10:34 AM
Peace = Staying centered as a part of the universe
Warmth = kindness
Wonderment = clouds in the sky
Love = Me (surrounded by 🥰🥰🥰)
Laughter = Joy
Peace = Staying centered as part of the universe
Present = Moment (step by step)
Moment = Breathless then light

Me trying to sort shit out is funny.
I'm glad I can bring myself humor.

DECEMBER 14, 2023
7:24 AM
Once I stopped trying to get everything back that I felt was taken from me, I was freed.

Letting someone misunderstand you can hinder the depth of your relationship. That is why living authentically is so important.

DECEMBER 16, 2023
6:17 AM
See between the lines and observe what has been hidden there all along.

DECEMBER 18, 2023
9:55 AM

Tap into a peaceful mindset and banish fear by crafting your story with love, abundance, and light. Shannon, don't forget to illuminate every room you enter with positivity.

Also, remember: You are always ready.

DECEMBER 23, 2023
8:52 PM

Why do we keep ourselves so busy?
Do we think that equals success?
If we're doing, are we really achieving?
What does action equal?
For me "today," it equals not forgetting.
Why is it that we are taught that just pausing, just breathing, just being present is not enough?

DECEMBER 29, 2023
3:43 AM

How is it that I can know my part, be my part in this moment?
It all happens for a reason.
The triumph and the tragedy.
They are all gifts in my journey.
What did it take for me to realize this truth?
What does it take for us all to realize our part?
How can we realize what life is trying to teach us?

Learn from what we are shown. Understand the meaning behind our experiences. Question what we need to learn from these moments. Explore the reasons for being exposed to new things.

Truth: Why do I truly avoid, not understand, despise, and get disappointed by some experiences?
Acceptance: What is this going to teach me?

> **I am made of stardust and grace. There is more than one way to open a new path.**
>
> – Shannon Michelle

Equality: Why do I need to learn this?
Guidance: What do I need to learn from this?
Joy: What truly do I gain from this?
Freedom: I am able to move on once I truly understand we are all equal.

I will be OK.

My story today: Amor fati is a Latin for "love of fate" or "love of one's fate." It is used to describe an attitude in which one sees everything that happens in one's life, including suffering and loss, as good or, at the very least, necessary.

6:56 AM
What are you looking for in your self-definition?
Why do you self-define?
Who are you trying to be?
I hear my mom self-define often.
Why?
How would you describe yourself?
I think we humans receive, reflect, then decide.

Carpe diem.

8:23 AM
Why does your anger or disappointment feel like it gives you strength?

DECEMBER 30, 2023
7:26 AM
The rain is pouring, washing away both love and sorrow.
Realize you still have chaos in yourself.
What is love?
What is creation?
A star is born: you.

I am writing to remind myself, to guide myself, to guide us all.
Because we are all one.

What changes me changes you.
Feeling loss and despair is a state of not knowing yourself and not trusting yourself.
Loss is part of the journey.
Despair is part of the journey.
Please do not try to lose despair; embrace it.
Treat despair and love in the same breath.
Both are equal, both are necessary for any sort of balance.

DECEMBER 31, 2023
6:12 AM
Stop comparing yourself to others.
We easily compare ourselves to others to find an easy way to see ourselves in a positive or negative way. My habit is to compare myself to people so that I can feel better about who I am. But that's just not the truth. The truth is we can only compare ourselves to ourselves. Others have nothing to do with who we are or where we want to see ourselves. Let's break free from comparison and stay in the moment. Comparing ourselves holds us back.

Stop comparing yourself to someone else to make yourself feel better in any way.

You are both wonderful individuals in different ways. That's the beauty.

DECEMBER 31, 2023
10:48 AM
Guidance was found in my body, my soul, and my mind. It has been a very bumpy road in my search for them. Many uphill climbs. Many roadblocks. But with the right guidance on tough roads, we make it through.

I've embraced so many moments on rebuilding my brain capacity and created a channel between me and my loved ones when they had no hope or idea of my return to this world.

JANUARY 3, 2024
12:23 PM
Transformed.
Embark on the quest to rediscover yourself.
Break open all your parts: good and bad.
Own them all.
Awaken yourself to become a whole person.
Stepping-stones.
Embrace your truest self, let go of fear, and live in the present.
Presents, patience, pleasure.

JANUARY 4, 2024
10:05 PM
My days feel like a rollercoaster of irony, where time flies by and things constantly change.
[Do you] ever wonder how it all seems to happen when you feel like you're doing nothing?

JANUARY 6, 2024
12:46 PM
Why do we believe that if we put in enough stressful energy, it might change things.

JANUARY 7, 2024
8:55 PM
Today was another unique day.
Sometimes, you can't realize how unique a day is until the end of it. It can be simple, playful, loving, or fearful.

But this is what popped out of my rebuilt brain: Why do you keep asking people to describe their feelings going through my trauma? That truly is not present, which, to me, is my most vital gift.

Trust yourself again.
Remember who you are and why it's so important for you to share your experiences.

> **The funny thing is you don't know what you don't know until you know.**
>
> – Shannon Michelle

Quit asking questions.
Just stay present.

And then that made me think: Why do we go through our lives not staying present?

Take it one step at a time.

JANUARY 9, 2024
9:44 AM
Now, I truly understand.
I said "I'm going to let you go," which was empowering for me to even look at our connection that way to see that I had the limitations/blocks, which felt like control.
Then I realized I was the one holding on, and that was me trying to guide my future. As silly as it all seems, we are on the same level and in each other's hearts, but we have different wants and needs.

Letting go is the only way to get what you want. Freedom comes from your inner strength.

JANUARY 12, 2024
8:23 PM
I have been rebirthed. I have been reborn. It also means that now, in one way or another, this body is a virgin again.

Post a very vibrant sexual life?
Post having a baby?
This mind and body have been reborn.

Also, many parts have been broken and put back together with new pieces.

All I know is that my body has not been sexually pleased for two years. A lot of crazy thoughts, but I'll also have a lot of realistic moments about my new existence.

What a gift to be able to share this body for the first time again.

JANUARY 26, 2024
7:58 PM
Our minds are entangled, they do not exist without experiences.

There is no experience in the brain.
There are no images in the brain.
There are no sounds in the brain.
There are no textures in the brain.
There are no thoughts in the brain.
There's nothing we can call an experience in the brain.
What we see is electrochemistry.
The brain is a modified source of consciousness.
The mind is not a "thing," it's consciousness.
The most important question is:
Who am I?

JANUARY 27, 2024
8:07 AM
Looking for the best words that describe my in-between state.
Nothingness sounds empty to me.

When in fact, I knew I was in full abundance.

JANUARY 29, 2024
8:41 PM
I'm scared.
I am lonely.
What's the difference between being scared versus lonely?
Afraid.
Tired.
Sad.
I am ready.
I am ready.
I am ready.

" Don't look at the past.

Don't hope for a future.

Be present.

To find pure joy...

just stay present. "

– Shannon Michelle

JANUARY 30, 2024
7:55 AM
Personal awakening.
Sometimes that seems possible, and sometimes that seems unbelievable.

JANUARY 30, 2024
10:55 AM
I'm breathless.
I'm sad.
I'm alone.
I don't remember how to get out of this mess. Where is my to-do list, because I need it, too.
This is a motherfucker.
Go fix yourself again, Shannon.
Everybody's done enough.
That is so not true.
We can't just fix ourselves.
We want to believe that, but that's just not the truth.
Find understanding.
Find gratitude.
Find yourself.

JANUARY 31, 2024
8:21 AM
She's back!
Almost two years ago, I was definitely broken and then reborn into the gorgeous, new Shannon Michelle, 2.0. Gratitude, gratitude, gratitude! A very slow journey but stepping into my own miracle.

FEBRUARY 1, 2024
7:42 AM
After a beautiful and in-depth conversation with my daughter, Grace, today, she asked me, "How are you feeling?" I said it's been hard these last few days. I have felt very confused and very lonely. As much as I appreciate my recovery, I don't want to return with some of the old traits that were not very helpful.

Vulnerability is a gift.

Loneliness is a fear. I'm trying to learn the difference between being vulnerable and feeling lonely. I think I used to confuse those two.

Vulnerability was a weakness—at least, that's what I thought. I now know that vulnerability is a gift, not a weakness. I do not want to lose the wisdom that I have gained.

One way I would fight against feeling afraid was through strength, which supposedly comes from not being vulnerable. I would fill every moment of my life to the fullest to avoid weakness. I realize that I left no space for the balancing of both sides.

Good and bad.
Strength and weakness.

You can't live a full life unless you're willing to embrace both sides.

FEBRUARY 2, 2024
8:13 AM

Hard day, hard week.

Try to remember to stay present.

Try to remember: patience, patience, patience.

Try to remember how strong you really are.

Try to remember it's OK to be alone.

Just try to remember the most important thing to do today is breathe.

You will be OK.

You will be great.

You've got this!

FEBRUARY 3, 2024
8:16 AM

Some days are just so hard because I am repeating the same mantra.

Gratitude for being alive. (Sometimes that just doesn't feel big enough.)

Sadness for being alone. (Sadness for feeling alone.)

I feel 50-50.

I don't have this fear that all men can hurt me any longer. Previously, I think I took the assumption that men could be awful people if I didn't

> " Sometimes you have to learn to live your life relying on your heart and soul more than you do your eyes. Insight is deeper than seeing. "

— Shannon Michelle

really know them. So, there were always boundaries and borders when getting to know me.

FEBRUARY 5, 2024
12:26 PM
I had a very good day.
No matter what you do as a mother, diaper phase, food, phase, relationship phase, trauma phase, Grace still loves me! No matter what. So grateful.

FEBRUARY 7, 2024
8:01 AM
The statement "the will of God" seems so limiting. Is there only one channel to receive? Only through your belief in God? Some of us use different descriptions, but we all mean the same thing.

FEBRUARY 8, 2024
3:04 PM
Why are the words "meditation" and "medication" so similar?

Give yourself the freedom to let go.
I want everything life has to give me.

FEBRUARY 10, 2024
12:39 PM
I asked my friend Elle, "From this experience, what did you gain or learn?" "Although, intellectually, I've known this already, I truly feel I learned emotionally that anything can happen to anyone at any moment. It can be a scary thought, but it just reminds me to never take the people I love in life for granted."

FEBRUARY 11, 2024
3:01 PM
Reality is that life is both "rough and hard" and "easy and smooth."
Stop trying to be on one side or the other.
Stay centered.

FEBRUARY 12, 2024
1:14 PM
Don't let the incident be the excuse.

Don't use one bad decision or traumatic moment to define you.
Use it, learn from it, and then move back into the presence of your existence.

Turn setbacks into stepping-stones. Learn from mistakes or tough times instead of letting them hold you back. Embrace the lessons, grow, and keep moving forward with confidence in your journey.

FEBRUARY 13, 2024
8:27 AM
Our childhood experiences allowed us to see the changes we wanted to make for ourselves.

Stay open and vulnerable.
You are worthy.
Stay present.
Stay present to stay aware that you are wanted and
Beautiful.
Worthy.
Needed.
Loved.
Sometimes you forget, and that's OK too.
Complete.

> "I died as a mineral and became a plant, I died as plant and became animal, I died as animal and I was human. Why should I fear? When was I less by dying?"
>
> – Rumi

emerging

It's wild what happens when you see death; your priorities dramatically shift, and things that used to be super important seem utterly stupid now.

— Shannon Michelle

LET'S GO BACK TO THAT DIARY ENTRY FROM APRIL 30, 2023, when I spoke those dreadful words into my phone that no woman wants to ever say: "I have breast cancer." Long before my accident, my doctor had been asking me to get a mammogram because of my age and previous findings. They had seen markers that initially made them think I had breast cancer years before, but the reports always came back negative. When it was time for my next mammogram, I had to keep postponing it due to my surgeries and other medical issues I was dealing with.

I kept telling my doctor that I would get a mammogram eventually, but I wanted to focus on healing from my extensive injuries. I remember asking, "How long can I wait?" They told me, "It's already been too long." So, I went for a mammogram.

When I got the results, the doctors said they saw something. I thought, "I'm OK. I've been through mammograms before. They're probably seeing something benign again." I figured they'd do the biopsy and tell me everything was fine, just like all the other times. When I received the phone call with my biopsy results, my doctor carefully told me I had breast cancer. To my surprise, I started laughing.

I thought, "If something were going to kill me, it wouldn't be cancer." Even when I found out I had breast cancer, I felt calm and collected. I believed that if my life were truly in danger, it would have already happened. Hanging up the phone, I laughed again, realizing it wasn't as terrible as I had imagined.

Determined to move forward, I scheduled the outpatient surgery for the first thing in the morning because I knew I couldn't eat or drink for twelve hours, so I wanted to get it over with, go home, and crawl back into bed with a warm cup of tea and a cookie.

A few days after the surgery, I got a call informing me that it was worse than the doctors had anticipated. They could only see a two centimeters lump on the X-rays. It didn't show that the cancer was attached to my implant, but once they were in, they realized it was bigger and more dangerous than they expected. My implant hid most of the cancer. My doctor couldn't remove the cancer without taking out my implant, and the hospital needed my permission to do that.

There was more cancer, and I needed to make decisions. That's when I freaked out. Even when they told me I had breast cancer, I couldn't focus on it because I was so focused on recovering from my brain and body traumas.

When my doctor asked if I wanted to remove just one implant and wait for my breast to heal before getting a new implant, I told him to take both out. I was done with surgeries. I wanted a break from being cut open.

My daughter emphasized, "Mom, you need to do the surgery now. It's not about what you're trying to fix from your motorcycle accident. You need to focus on your cancer. That's a bigger deal."

Within a week, two surgeons coordinated to perform the second surgery. The plastic surgeon removed the implants, and the oncologist took out the remaining cancer. Since the cancer had metastasized to my lymph nodes, they needed to remove some of those as well.

Initially, they thought the two surgeries would be enough, but it became more complicated. They needed additional tests to decide between chemotherapy and radiation. This process took several weeks. Finally, during a phone conversation, I learned that I would only need radiation, which felt so much easier than chemo.

I went from saying "I'm fine, nothing's wrong. Everything is good" to realizing it was a mess. I began to think, "How do I fix this problem, this trauma? How do I address this issue?"

I was relieved that I didn't have to undergo chemotherapy. My first reaction was, "That's good; it's just radiation." But then I started to feel scared about how the radiation would affect me.

What bothered me even more was the daily logistics. I hated the idea of needing to be taken to my radiation appointments every day for six weeks. It meant someone had to come over, and that dependency stressed me out more than the treatments themselves. Relying on others for my well-being wasn't something I wanted to impose on people daily. They had just gone through a year of hell with me: now this?

My main concern wasn't the radiation, but the burden I felt I'd be placing on others. My daughter, Grace, took me to my appointments for the first three weeks. She drove me there and patiently waited for me, then got me home and in bed, even though she needed to be back in college.

It was hard asking others for help every day. My doctors even suggested I stay in an apartment nearby so I could walk to my appointments, but I wanted to sleep in my own bed after radiation treatments. I don't remember everything clearly, but I recall feeling overwhelmed at first and then completely exhausted.

I just kept looking forward to the day it would all be over. I repeatedly asked, "Once I finish this, will I be done with cancer?" Between the motorcycle accident and then the breast cancer, I was depleted and covered in scars.

The irony is that I placed massive self-worth on my appearance before all this craziness. I had fallen into the trap of believing that a woman's attractiveness was largely determined by how perky her breasts were. Although I might have denied it at the time, my decision to get breast implants was driven by this flawed belief.

I have always had a fantastic body. However, after giving birth to my daughter, I found myself grappling with insecurities about my post-breastfeeding body. A few years later, Brian and I broke up. That only added to my feelings of inadequacy. There I was, a single mom with sagging breasts, thinking that this one physical attribute I had always been proud of was now gone.

I thought that I was not *wantable* because of the way I looked after giving birth. I had to fix it and be more *wantable*, so that Brian would stay with me. I didn't understand why I wasn't enough. I

> " Now, I see my scars as a road map of my crazy journey from death to life, and I am proud of every single one of them. "
>
> — Shannon Michelle

" I transformed from someone who tried to control every aspect of life to someone who embraces vulnerability and the unpredictability of out-comes. Before the accident, the idea of being "breakable" felt unbearable. Ironically, I had to break to discover my beautiful strength and vulnerability. "

— Shannon Michelle

assumed making physical changes would make me more *wantable,* so I got a boob job.

When Grace was still young, I met with a plastic surgeon to discuss my options to get back my perky pre-pregnancy breasts, I was given two choices. The first option involved extensive cutting and scarring, while the second was to insert implants that would fill out my sagging skin, leaving almost no scars. I went with option two. The irony doesn't escape me now. I was hiding behind a distorted sense of self, thinking that implants could make me a better, more attractive person without any visible scars. It's sad I gave so much value to such bullshit.

I don't remember telling anyone about my breast implants—much like how I chose to keep silent about my chaotic childhood and the sexual abuse I endured. Even my own daughter was unaware of my past or my implants. It felt like just another piece of my life that I preferred to keep in the shadows.

At the core of my brain trauma, I had to rebuild neural connections as well as my personal history. This process involved slowly reliving my life to remember who I was. My memories came to me from what I remembered as a kid moving forward, not as an adult going backward. Going through this experience of remembering, I realized that I forgot almost everything I experienced as a child.

Rebuilding my brain and relearning my life started with remembering my childhood.

The brain trauma I suffered brought back memories I had previously buried for my own protection, and I realized that I needed to explore my past. Before the accident, I did a great job hiding my childhood trauma, but my new brain wasn't going to hold onto painful secrets any longer. The truth was emerging from the shattered corners of my memory like a prism.

I was raised by alcoholic parents who couldn't control their wants and needs. This abuse created a level of insecurity in my life that included questioning my worth and the way I presented myself to the outside world.

Seeing my childhood through my broken brain, I recognized the appalling level of abuse I withstood. I was tossed around, sexually molested, and shoveled in and out of homes, caregivers, and schools. My parents' struggles with addiction left them unable to manage their own needs, which only amplified my insecurities. This chaotic environment made me question my self-worth. I wanted to be loved; I wanted to be wanted; I wanted to be seen. Now I understand that getting breast implants was a way that I thought that my inner child would be noticed.

This new Shannon 2.0 views beauty differently than Shannon 1.0 did. The old Shannon tied her self-worth to her appearance and the world's perception of her. Now, I don't care how the world sees me; what matters is how I see myself. I accept myself for who I truly am—with all my lumps, bumps, scars, and even my cross-eyed gaze—and I love her!

Letting go of the stigmas that weigh us down may be liberating. For me, it was my looks.

Despite how utterly messy my motorcycle accident/breast cancer rollercoaster ride was, the experience gave me a profound sense of freedom and joy.

In the end, I realized that true self-worth comes from within. It's not about how you look on the outside, but how you feel about yourself on the inside. My journey taught me that confidence and beauty are not defined by physical attributes, but by the strength, resilience, and love we carry within us.

I made a lot of money making things look amazing. I was very good at creating beauty, including making my body look attractive. I was told to remove the cancer, it made sense to eliminate something that could harm me. But when you're asked to change things about yourself, it can feel excruciating.

Being challenged with something so severe in my life taught me a valuable lesson. I had reached a point where I felt like nothing bad could happen anymore because I had already endured so much. But the experience of facing breast cancer showed me that life doesn't have an end game for its challenges. There's no such thing as having experienced enough or done enough. Life constantly presents us with both good and bad moments.

This realization was a gift. It forced me to see myself as vulnerable again. I thought I had dealt with everything one person could possibly endure, but I had to be torn open, and more of my issues had to emerge.

The universe shows us that life will constantly change and differ from what we assume. Until we accept that nothing stays the same, we haven't truly learned the lesson that trauma is meant to teach us.

rebooting

Although no one can go back and make a brand new start, anyone can start from now and make a brand new ending.

– Carl Bard

WITH THE EMOTION, PHYSICAL AND MENTAL TRAIN wreck from the accident, and the dumpster fire from cancer, I had to find consistency in my life. Since I spent so many mornings waking up wondering what just happened and where the hell I was at, I had to put into place some practices that supported my brain's rebooting process. Yep, life after experiencing a painful event or traumatic brain injury (TBI) sucks. It can be a confusing journey filled with challenges, uncertainties, and "holy crap" moments.

Grappling with memory loss and the relentless quest to find clarity amid the chaos is a pain, so I've created some rebooting practices to help you restore your sense of peace in these super crazy times.

You are not alone on this journey. Together, let's explore these strategies that will help you emerge stronger, more self-aware, and resilient in the face of adversity.

- Create Space for Healing
- Embracing and Conquering Fear
- Learning to Detach from Your Pain
- Finding Balance

PRACTICE ONE

Create Space for Healing

When life throws you a curveball—be it heartbreak, mental stress, or physical setbacks—it can feel overwhelming. However, such challenges offer a unique opportunity to build strength and resilience. When my life abruptly stopped, I had the chance to think about what I needed to reboot. Creating a safe space at home was challenging but transformational. It allowed me to heal and reconnect with myself. This experience taught me how to cultivate an environment that fosters recovery, personal growth, and self-discovery.

Creating a physical and mental space dedicated to your healing can provide the grounding you need to start the process.

Step 1: Find a Place to Call Your Own

Find a spot in your home where you feel safe and comfortable. This place could be a corner of a room, a favorite chair, or even a small outdoor area. My space overlooks the backyard where bird feeders and chimes create a symphony of nature. When I look outside, I see the beauty which helps me connect to the healing energies within me.

Step 2: Clear the Energy

Before you settle into your space, clear any negative energy. This can be done through smudging with sage, playing calming music, or simply decluttering the area to create a sense of openness and tranquility. I open a window, burn sage, or light a candle before settling into my space.

Step 3: Fill Your Space with Things That Bring You Joy

Surround yourself with items that uplift your spirits. This may include cherished mementos, plants, or artwork that inspires you. In my sanctuary, I surround myself with crystals and stones that make me smile when I see them.

Step 4: Make It Cozy

Comfort is key to feeling safe and secure. Add soft blankets, cushions, or anything else that makes your space inviting and warm. I have a few pillows that support my head, a cozy throw, and some slippers.

Step 5: Find Time to Go There Regularly

Make time to go there daily, whether for meditation, breathing, or simply sitting in silence. Honestly, just breathing was painful, so be gentle with yourself. For weeks, I just sat and tried to stay present; after a few months, I was able to read. Now, I keep a collection of books within reach, finding inspiration in quotes that encourage self-reflection and personal growth.

Step 6: Create a Ritual

Establish a simple ritual you can perform each time you enter your healing space. Consistency will help reinforce this as a safe haven. When I get ready to settle into my healing space, I put on my robe, even if I have clothes on. Repeating my routine brings me some normalcy and comfort when everything—including my brain—seems so broken.

Step 7: Practice Self-Compassion

Be gentle with yourself. Acknowledge your feelings, both physical and emotional, without judgment and allow yourself to experience them fully when in your space. This act of self-compassion is a powerful tool in your healing journey. Remember, healing is not linear, and it's OK to have setbacks.

PRACTICE TWO

Embracing and Conquering Fear

Fear is a natural part of life. We all encounter it, but sometimes it feels overwhelming and paralyzing. However, fear may become a gift because it tells us when something in our life is out of balance or we're not prioritizing ourselves.

Fear sat with me for so long, but today, I can face it head-on. It no longer scares me. My first step in overcoming it was to stop taking responsibility for everything. Often, our anxieties stem from trying to control everything around us. When I realized this, I began to release that need for control.

Step 1: Get Present

Fear often pulls us into the past or pushes us into the future. Staying present is the antidote. Whenever I felt fearful, I reminded myself to stay in the moment. Focusing on my surroundings helped me process and move through fear. I would look out the window and watch the playful birds or listen to calming music. This practice kept me grounded and free from the constant fear of what I had lost or what the future might hold.

Step 2: Breathe

This helps calm your nervous system and brings clarity to your thoughts. Deliberate breathing forces me to stay present with my breath. There is nowhere else I can be when I focus on inhaling and exhaling.

Close your eyes and take a slow, deep breath through your nose for a count of three. Hold your breath for a count of three. Exhale slowly through your mouth for a count of three. Repeat this cycle several times until you feel more centered and calmer.

When I first started this practice, my brain was in so much pain that breathing was super tough and I couldn't make it the full three seconds.

Step 3: Embrace Change

My life post-accident was vastly different from before. Instead of resisting these changes, I learned to embrace each moment of my present life, understanding that it was different but still valuable. This shift in perspective helped reduce my fear. I was not the same person that I was before my accident, and trying to find her was a waste of time, so I accepted the new me and learned to trust her.

Step 4: Release the Need for Control

Much of our fear comes from thinking we can control everything. By letting go of this need, I found peace. I learned it was OK not to have all the answers or control over every situation. Now, when things get super overwhelming and fearful, I fall into my surroundings, instead of trying to control my thoughts. I open myself to the whispers of the world around me. I listen to the gentle rustle of the wind, the songs of birds in the trees, and the quiet wisdom of my spirit guides. I sit in stillness, offering my full presence, and simply listen.

Step 5: Find a Place of Non-Judgment

I had a lot of crap to process, but finding grace in the chaos helped ease my anxiety. It's OK to feel fear—it's a natural human emotion. Avoid labeling your feelings as "good" or "bad." Instead, observe your emotions as they come and go, like clouds passing in the sky. Be kind and gentle with yourself as you explore these feelings.

Step 6: Be Thankful for the Wins

When you shift your focus from fear to gratitude, it opens space for peace and appreciation. I would think of my amazing daughter, beautiful home, and caring friends.

I invite you to reflect on recent moments that brought you happiness, such as a meal with a friend, a hot cup of tea, or a lazy day on the couch watching silly movies. Send a silent thank you to each person or event you are grateful for. When I got better at remembering, I would go through the alphabet and find something to be grateful for with each letter. It could be as simple as the crunchy, sweet A-apple I ate, the warm B-bath I took, my loving C-cat, etc.

Step 7: Honor Your Progress

Celebrate the steps you've taken to face your fears. This gives you a sense of achievement and helps reduce your anxiety. I found that small victories, like going to the bathroom alone, were big wins for me.

Take a moment to appreciate each improvement. Look back at where you started and be grateful for how far you've come. If you have setbacks, view them as learning experiences, not failures. You can track your progress by taking photos, journaling, or recording your thoughts.

Fear is a part of life, but it doesn't have to rule our lives. By staying present, understanding the true source of our fears, embracing change, and releasing the need for control, we can transform fear into a powerful gift that guides us to live more fully. Remember, it's a journey, and taking it one step at a time is OK. You're not alone, and you have the strength within you to overcome fear.

Stay present, and you'll find peace.

PRACTICE THREE

Learning to Detach from Your Pain

My deep healing began when I acknowledged and accepted my pain, which enabled me to start detaching from it. Please recognize that the pain or trauma you're experiencing is a part of your personal history, but it does not define you. The goal of this process is to separate yourself from your trauma, allowing you to move forward without constant worry.

Step 1: Know What You Can Control

After waking from the coma, there was little in my life that I could control, including my bladder. Slowly, I was able to learn how to control my body, but that didn't stop the pain from overtaking me. I had to learn to accept what was within my control.

So, the first step to detaching is identifying the aspects of your life and situations you can influence. Recognize that while you cannot change the past, you have the power to shape your present and future. Doing this helped me to separate what I went through from who I truly am.

Step 2: Accept That Pain Does Not Define You

While my friends and family would come and go, pain was my only steady companion for months. We all encounter experiences that shape us, some of which cause massive pain and trauma.

Your identity is separate from the trauma you have endured. Recognize that your experiences and pain are just parts of your story. They may inform certain aspects of your life, but they do not have the power to dictate your entire identity. Distinguishing yourself from the trauma you've faced is a significant step in reclaiming your sense of self.

I won't let the motorcycle accident define who I am. So, to remind myself of that, I repeat mantras like, "I am strong," "I am valuable," and "I am more than my past." These affirmations can reinforce your inner strength and shift your mindset towards a more empowered version of yourself.

Step 3: Manage Your Expectations

Being the type A person that I was before my accident, parts of me got tired of not healing faster. I would get so frustrated with myself, and that was not healthy. I had to understand in my healing journey there would be ups and downs, and I had to be gentle with myself. So, I set realistic milestones and celebrated small victories. With the help of my doctors, we created a plan with achievable, short-term, and long-term goals, like taking a walk down my street every day. It's important to allow yourself grace and patience when setbacks occur.

Step 4: Embrace Change and Uncertainty

I spent so long clinging to the person I believed I was before the accident that I never allowed myself the opportunity to transform. It was only when I acknowledged that change is a natural part of the healing process that a new version of me began to emerge. By accepting Shannon 2.0, I was able to release Shannon 1.0.

Step 5: Set Boundaries

The first person I needed to set boundaries with was myself. Whenever I pushed myself too hard, it would result in a splitting headache or overwhelming body pain. I had to learn to say "no" to myself: for example, "No, I won't move this bookshelf." This practice allowed me to confidently set boundaries with situations and people that drained my energy or hindered my healing process. Prioritize your well-being by establishing clear personal and emotional boundaries with yourself and others.

Recognize your own limits and make self-care a priority. Establishing personal and emotional boundaries isn't just about protecting your physical well-being; it's about nurturing every aspect of your health. You deserve to thrive, so start by setting those essential boundaries today.

Step 6: Let Go of Things, People, and Thoughts That Don't Serve Your Healing

The most challenging thing for me to let go of was thoughts that didn't serve me, like "I should be doing better" and "Why me?" Once I stopped the noise, I could detach from my own doubt and release attachments to negative thoughts and unproductive habits. Understand that letting go is a step toward making space for positive growth.

Step 7: Reflect and Learn

In my safe space, I reflected on my healing progress and the lessons I learned. I kept reminding myself to use my experiences to grow and build a stronger, more resilient self. If I did something that caused me pain, I would figure out a way to do it that was pain-free. If I had negative thoughts, I would counter them with positive affirmations from the many books by my bed.

Each day is an opportunity to reflect and learn.

Your healing journey is deeply personal and unique to you. By following these practices, you'll gradually let go of the trauma and move toward a more peaceful and empowered state. If you need additional support, consider finding a therapist to guide you. Remember, there is no straight path to healing, so be kind to yourself and celebrate every victory.

PRACTICE FOUR

Finding Balance

Balance was a big thing for me. When I gained consciousness, I could not stand, let alone walk. My world was so whack-a-doodle that it took me a while to understand the importance of balance.

Once I was able to find balance in my body, I realized that I had to find emotional balance. Finding balance involves courage, self-awareness, and a willingness to confront both the light and dark aspects of yourself. This practice will take you through key steps to create balance in your life, helping you to integrate all parts of your being and move forward with greater wholeness.

My whole life I strived to focus on only the good, denying the bad. But I've learned that I need to be open to both sides if I want to heal and grow. I found that, to find balance, it's really important to recognize and accept both positive and negative aspects of my life and self.

This means being open to:

- **Good & Bad:** Acknowledge that life is a mix of highs and lows. Every positive experience may have its challenges, and every difficult moment can bring valuable lessons. Once I accepted this truth, when I had crappy days, I knew that I would have a good day soon.

- **Success & Failure:** Understand that success is not a straight path. Celebrate your achievements, but also learn to see failure as an opportunity for growth. I recognized that my failures were opportunities to learn. At first, that was a lesson.
- **Love & Hate:** Allow yourself to feel deep emotions, both positive and negative. Both love and hate can teach you important truths about your values and boundaries.
- **Strength & Weakness:** Recognize your strengths and use them, but don't ignore your weaknesses. Working on your weaknesses can make you stronger overall.
- **Confidence & Neediness:** It's OK to be confident in some areas and needy in others. Accepting this duality may help you seek support when needed and stand firm when required. I hated being needy, but when I reached out for help, there was always someone there to care for me. It was tough, but through my vulnerability, I found my strength.

These rebooting exercises have been my lifeline through pain, trauma, and the tangled web of my memory challenges. I hope they bring you the same clarity and peace they've given me. If you need additional support on your healing journey, please don't hesitate to seek medical attention.

Now that you have a few practices you can tune into when you need some rebooting, I want to share with you a simple acronym I created to use anytime I've started to feel bad. I call it my LOVE BATH, and it helps me get centered when everything around me seems to be off-balance.

LOVE BATH

The acronym LOVE BATH refers to two things that bring me much joy:
1. Feeling loved
2. A relaxing bath.

I chose these words, so you could easily remember these strategies to help you cope, heal, and grow.

LOVE
Trauma, in all its many forms, really sucks. Sure, I suffered a boatload of trauma as a child, but it didn't break me open like this round of physical trauma did. Hopefully, with the help of this book, you'll be able to use my insights to get you through your trauma with triumph and forgo any super painful events.

L - Let Go
O - Open Up
V - Vulnerability Is Key
E - Embrace Each Emotion

B - Be Present
A - Ask, Listen, and Answer
T - Time Wins: Patience
H - Have Faith

L - Let Go
Holding onto anger, frustration, or sadness may hinder recovery and your ability to heal, be it physical or emotional. It's vital to acknowledge your emotions and learn how to release them. You

need to name it to claim it, even emotions we don't want to admit feeling. Techniques like journaling, meditation, and talking to a therapist may help this process.

It's natural to feel like you lost something huge—you did! The first thing I had to let go of was whoever I was before the accident. I felt a lot of jealousy for Shannon 1.0 and her fun-filled life. I would tell myself, "She was amazing, but I'm not." I had to let that story go. It was not true and didn't serve me.

Now it's time to let go of any resentment you feel toward yourself and others, because letting go opens up space for healing and discoveries.

O - Open Up

Being open and honest about your situation is key. Openness fosters understanding and ensures you receive the support you need. Be honest with yourself and others about your thoughts and experiences, including the ones that suck.

Open communication builds trust for you and those who are helping you. First, I opened up to the nurses, letting them know my needs. It might sound obvious to the outside world, but letting someone know I had to go to the bathroom and needed help was huge for me. Doing so literally got me out of my own crap.

V - Vulnerability Is Key

Vulnerability isn't a sign of weakness; it's a path to genuine connections and healing. For most of my life, I avoided being vulnerable. But after my accident, I had to rely on those around me. This experience revealed how many people were there to help and how loved I truly was.

If you're going through trauma, remember it's OK to be vulnerable. We all need help sometimes. Reaching out benefits you and brings joy to those who offer their support.

E - Embrace Each Emotion

Every emotion you experience is valid and part of your healing process. Instead of suppressing your feelings, allow yourself to experience them fully.

I expressed mine by talking into my phone. I spoke freely about how I was honestly feeling. Now, I look back on those recordings as tangible signs of progress.

Be open by sharing your story, and show vulnerability by letting others in. This is how we create true connections, healing, and love.

BATH
B - Be Present

Focus on the here and now. Breathing is an excellent way of staying focused on the present.

The reboots left me confused and frustrated. When I accepted that the reboots would happen, I gave myself grace and breathed through each moment.

A - Ask, Listen, and Answer

So many things may be confusing after going through trauma, and communication involves asking for what you need and listening to what you want.

In the past, I would say "yes" to everything, regardless of how tired I felt or how full my plate was. Not anymore.

Now, I use the YES, NO, MAYBE framework to clarify my needs and boundaries. I will sit with the question and let my body answer it. YES means YES, NO means NO, and MAYBE is a NO I haven't committed to yet.

Ask yourself the question you want the answer to, say each word out loud, "yes," "no," or "maybe," and feel how your body responds. You will always get the correct answer if you take the time to settle into the question and allow the answer to flow to you.

T - Time Wins: Patience

Healing takes time. Be patient with yourself and those around you. Recognize that progress may be slow and celebrate small victories along the way. If you're like me, you want things to be done now, but brain injuries and trauma don't work that way. Stay present and find gratitude in that moment.

H - Have Faith

Belief is a powerful tool. Whether believing in your treatment plan, your body's ability to heal, or a higher power, having faith may provide comfort and strength. Trust the process, have faith in your resilience, and know that you have the power to overcome any challenge.

For me, I had faith that I was given this trauma as a gift. It was a gift I was going to learn from to share what I learned with others.

I have faith that what I went through will help you!

Living with a brain injury or trauma sucks, but with the right strategies and support, you can reclaim your life and find unexpected joys through the journey. Remember the LOVE BATH principles as you continue your journey. You are taking proactive steps toward managing and thriving despite your trauma or brain injuries.

SOME HELPFUL ADVICE FOR CAREGIVERS

This section is specifically for those caring for someone with traumatic brain injury or memory loss.

Through my experience, I want to help caregivers understand and manage the complexities of memory impairment with grace, patience, and love.

Respect the Repeats: One of the most common challenges you'll face as a caregiver is repetitive questions or stories. While it can be frustrating, it's important to remember:

- **Stay patient:** Take a deep breath and answer each question as if it were the first time.
- **Show interest:** Engage in the conversation even if you've heard the story multiple times. Talking with them helps your loved one feel valued.
- **Use positive reinforcement:** Respond with kindness and positivity to make the experience comforting for both parties.

The Unknowns Are Normal

Memory impairment may cause a lot of uncertainty, but understanding that "unknowns" are a part of the process will help you cope better:

- **Acknowledge the fear:** Both you and your loved one may feel scared or anxious about the unknown. It's OK to express these feelings, but I suggest you share them with someone else. It's too much to expect that your loved one who has a brain injury will understand what you're going through when they can't even understand what is happening to them.
- **Stay flexible:** Plans may change, and that's perfectly normal. Adaptability is your friend.

- **Focus on the present:** Help your loved one stay connected to the current moment to alleviate anxiety.

Be Patient

Patience is crucial when caring for someone with memory impairment. Remember:

- **Take breaks:** Caregiving is exhausting. Make sure to schedule regular breaks for yourself and be patient with yourself.
- **Show kindness:** Be kind to yourself first and recognize that this is hard work. It might feel like you are pushing the same heavy boulder up a hill, and your loved one might only remember some of your efforts. I get it.
- **Watch your tone:** The way you speak is just as important as what you say:
- **Use a gentle voice:** A calm, soothing tone may prevent agitation and confusion. I remember when friends would visit and I would share something I shared a million times before, but I didn't remember sharing. They got snarky with me a few times, which shut me down.
- **Avoid frustration:** If you feel frustrated, step away to collect yourself before continuing the conversation.

Record Everything

I wish my friends and family had taken more photos and videos of me on this journey. Keeping detailed records and photos will help everyone involved keep track of important information:

- **Take photos and videos:** Sometimes, the only proof of improvement comes from pictures and videos.
- **Use a journal:** Document daily activities, moods, and any changes in behavior. My uncle did this for me, and I can look

back and see my progress in a new light. Reading it is very encouraging.

- **Maintain medical records:** Keep all medical documents and appointments organized and accessible. I couldn't do this for myself, and now it's nearly impossible to find when and where I had specific procedures.

Love Is Key

Love guided me through this trauma: the self-love I cultivated and the unwavering support from others were my saving grace. Your small acts of love and kindness mean the world to people suffering from memory loss and trauma.

- **Show affection:** Simple gestures like holding hands or giving a hug go a long way.
- **Express gratitude:** Regularly tell your loved one how much they mean to you.
- **Be respectful:** Treating your loved one with dignity and respect is vital, even in difficult moments.
- **Be empathetic:** Try to understand what they might be feeling.
- **Stay positive:** Focus on the good moments and celebrate small victories.

Caring for a loved one with memory loss or brain injury is tough, but it can deepen emotional bonds. I remember feeling truly loved when others cared for me during my recovery. Their kindness helped me heal and rediscover my strengths.

Taking each day with patience and understanding may make a world of difference for your loved one having a tough time. Hang in there, stay compassionate, and keep the hope alive. You're doing a fantastic job!

being

You don't have to continue to struggle to be better and better and better. You are perfect in this moment, just being.

— Shannon Michelle

I FEEL LIKE THERE ARE TWO DIFFERENT SHANNONS. One made a conscious effort to return to a body demolished on the Pacific Coast Highway and is going through the restoration process of becoming a full functioning human being. There's also the Shannon who's all-knowing, quiet, and peaceful. She's the calm Shannon flying above it all; she sees her life as an expansive journey that didn't begin at her birth and is not going to end with a physical death.

" Trauma in its many forms sucks, regardless of the type of trauma that you experienced. You are not the same as you were before it happened. "

– Shannon Michelle

That Shannon is bigger, part of the vastness of the universe. I can feel the difference between knowing that I'm in this constricted body which has weight and all the physical manifestations that come with it—like pain as well as pleasure—and knowing that my identity is part of a timeless being who is not tied to the heaviness of daily life drama.

During my coma, I took a bit of eternity and brought it into my life. When I was floating in that other world, I saw what the universe was like, and it was so massive and loving that we could never imagine it from our earthly point-of-view. So, the key for me is to find moments in my day to reconnect with the oneness we are all a part of and savor the knowing that everything is going to be OK.

Sometimes, we need to close our eyes, center ourselves, and connect with the spiritual world. For me, that entails not getting distracted by the chaos of colors, sounds, and people. I never imagined that closing my eyes and just being would be such a powerful place.

For a short time between my life and death, I observed how everything is perceived and experienced through more than just our physical senses. It's about connecting with the spirit beyond our sensory experiences. This connection is empowering and represents a new version of myself. However, it doesn't happen every day. Sometimes, I struggle not to be distracted by everything around me. But I can regain my balance when I remember to close my eyes and not try to experience things through my senses. I can regain my strength and insightfulness, and that is beyond words.

After my accident, I emerged as a different person. I still carry much of who I was before, yet I can feel the growth and transformation within me. My changes were hard for many of the people around me because they lost the Shannon Michelle they loved. That's why I want to do my best to explain what it's like to experience such a huge

"Recognize that there are two parts of us, the light and the dark, the earthly and the eternal. Both are important."

– Teresa Rodriguez

shift. I can only tell you what I went through and how it affected me. My values, priorities, and desires are not the same as they were, and that can be tough for others to understand. For example, I used to love getting all dolled up and going out, now my looks are not a priority. I don't care how others see me anymore, because I see true self. I tell my friends that the Shannon they loved is still here, she just doesn't give a shit anymore about how other perceive her. For some of my friends, that was not good enough. They wanted the Shannon 1.0 who cared too much, showed up all the time, and made sure everything was perfect. Guess what? She's gone!

When I started feeling mentally stronger, I realized I was still clinging to fears and worries from my past. Much of my anxiety was caused by how people around me reacted to my changes. Some couldn't handle the new me, and I had to understand that was not my problem to solve. It was important for me to identify what parts of myself I wanted to keep and what parts to leave behind. I chose to leave behind those parts of me that felt unworthy, not good enough, and unloved.

Coming back into my rebooted brain profoundly shifted my perspective. It changed how I saw myself, envisioned my future, and treated others. I felt like two people at once—one navigating the challenges of this new life and the other quietly observing from a distance. This dual perspective gave me a chance to grow and learn, reminding me that we all have something to teach and learn from one another, even when the "other" is just a different version of ourselves.

I've noticed that the things which used to bug me no longer hold the same power. I don't take things personally anymore. I want to explain this in a way that people can understand, especially those who have never experienced a traumatic brain injury or memory loss.

" Facing a near-death experience and complete brain shutdown was a tough way to get my priorities and values in order, but it worked! "

— Shannon Michelle

Now I live my life in a place of peaceful confidence. After going through the hellhole I did, it's easy for me to find the effortless beauty in life. I don't need to endlessly improve myself. I can reinvent who I am, and that's powerful. This new version of me exists whether others like her or not.

Before my accident, I realized that I didn't truly trust myself. My sense of self was influenced by how others perceived me, rather than how I saw myself. So, I spent my life constantly seeking external validation. This transformation hasn't been easy, but it's been incredibly rewarding. Each day, I approach life with presence, thoughtfulness, and kindness toward myself. This is a huge shift from my previous mindset, in which I believed I could fix everything and that perfection was the goal. I no longer see life through the lens of doing things "right" or "better". Now, I focus on simply being.

This new attitude has given me the freedom to live each moment authentically, without the pressure of perfection. It's a gift to show up every day as I am, and it's a way of living that has brought me immense peace and self-confidence. When I think about how my values have shifted, the first thing that comes to mind is that I now prioritize myself more than I used to. I've learned to put myself first, something I never felt capable of doing before.

In the past, I didn't appreciate myself as much as I do now. Before, putting myself first felt selfish to me—like I was taking something away from others. I used to think, "If I put myself first, I'm being selfish. I should never do that." But now, I've come to realize that's not true.

From my perspective, my mindset has evolved significantly, especially in how I speak to myself and take care of my needs. In the past, I believed success was defined by my achievements rather than just being. I thought that if I performed well enough, I could

" Valuing myself doesn't mean others lose out; it means I have more to give.

– Shannon Michelle

achieve success which I equated with having a nice home, a nice car, and financial stability.

Today, I realize that, while those experiences shaped who I am, they do not define my value. My true worth lies in who I am at this very moment—engaging in conversations with friends, interacting with others, and living my life on a day-to-day basis. Understanding this has allowed me to see my intrinsic value and to recognize that I am only responsible for myself.

Previously, I carried the burden of thinking I could create success for others through my actions, which, in hindsight, was an unrealistic expectation. Now, I understand that my responsibility is to myself, and that is where my focus shall remain.

So how do you get there without experiencing massive brain trauma, near death experience, breast cancer, and a coma? Begin by taking small steps to recognize your value. It's essential to understand that your worth isn't defined by what you do, but by who you are. When you stop measuring yourself solely by your actions, it becomes incredibly empowering. Prioritize yourself, peeling back the layers of doubt and societal expectations. Show up for yourself first, and you'll discover profound personal empowerment and self-worth.

Start by establishing a ritual that prioritizes valuing yourself. Begin each morning by taking a moment to breathe deeply and focus on self-care. This simple act of creating a pause in your day allows you to give yourself the time to breathe, observe, and just be. By putting yourself first and taking this pause, you enable yourself to move forward as the best version of yourself for others. Remember, this will look and feel different each day, and that's perfectly OK.

When you finish this book, I hope you take away a deeper understanding of the universal struggles we all face. By sharing the true difficulties of my own journey, I aim to show that we are all in this together. Life is challenging for everyone, but there are always moments of kindness and softness, no matter what. My hope is that this book helps you see yourself with greater love, patience, and clarity.

I encourage you to embrace vulnerability as a strength, rather than a weakness. It is in our openness and authenticity that we find true connection with others. Remember, each challenge is an opportunity for growth, pushing us to evolve and adapt. Life's unpredictability may be daunting, but it is also what makes it beautiful and worth living. As you navigate your personal path, may you find inspiration and courage in knowing that every step, no matter how small, contributes to your unique story. So, step into your miracle.

"Taking the time to pause and prioritize self-care allows you to fully participate in your own life, which is ultimately the best way to show up for others."

— Shannon Michelle

resources for recovery

There's a lot to forget. Trust me.

— Shannon Michelle

IN MY OWN HEALING JOURNEY, I'VE FOUND THAT focusing on three vital areas—brain, body, and spirit—has been incredibly beneficial. Whether it's engaging in mindfulness practices, undergoing physical rehabilitation, or nurturing your spiritual growth, there are many paths to consider. Remember, you're not alone in this. There are support networks and guidance available for caregivers, too, ensuring they have the tools needed to tackle the emotional and practical challenges of supporting a loved one. You've got this!

BRAIN

In the beginning, I relied on visuals to help me relearn and make sense of things. I would look at photos, observe my surroundings at home, and explore my collection of books, even if I couldn't read them. Rediscovering the familiar was a vital part of my healing process.

The beginning of my brain recovery was supported by the amazing work of Kevin Pearce, who started LoveYourBrain. They offer online classes, including meditation, yoga rehabilitation, and therapy. They also host in-person retreats twice a year. You can find more resources at LoveYourBrain.com.

Flipbooks and Photo Albums

Flipbooks were an easy and positive way to relearn without too much stress. I could recognize words when only a few were on a page with color and images. Each new day, I would wake up and flip open a book to a random page and read its message to me without overthinking it. Sometimes, I had to look up words, but it was a great way to engage my brain without overwhelming it. Photo albums also helped me to reconnect with my past. I could take my time and look at pictures, which helped me remember my memories.

FlipBooks

You Are Strong Hallmark flipbook with empowering sayings
  • I use this in different places around my house. I liked it as the first thing I saw in the morning in my kitchen.
Word of the Day flipbook
  • Even when I couldn't read, I would try to figure out what the word was.

Books

The Little Book of Light by Mikaela Katherine Jones
- Each day I opened the book to a random a page, try to read what it said, and mark the date.

Prescriptions for Happiness by Ken Keyes, Jr.
- When I got better at reading, I skimmed through this book to find passages that resonated with me.

The Boy, the Mole, the Fox and the Horse by Charlie Mackesy
- This is a sweet book that brought a smile to my face.

The Tao of Pooh by Benjamin Hoff
- It reminded me how important it is to stay close to the child within us.

Audiobooks

When reading was impossible, I would spend my days listening to audiobooks. I learned so much from these books. Many I have listened to a few times. Find books that resonate with you or listen to some of my favorites:

The Body Keeps Score by Bessel van der Kolk
- This book reminded me that my body suffered a lot of traumas and to be patient with my recovery.

Atlas of the Heart by Brené Brown
- This book taught me that all my emotions are valid and everything we feel is fair—good and bad.

The Sound of a Wild Snail Eating by Elisabeth Tova Bailey
- A gentle reminder that everything takes time and things will be okay in the end.

The One-Minute Cure by Madison Cavanaugh
- A short book that explains how oxygen and cancer can't live in the same space.

True Grit and Grace: Turning Tragedy Into Triumph by Amberly Lago
- This is about a woman who went through a motorcycle accident similar to mine and how she made it through her trauma.

The Four Agreements by Don Miguel Ruiz
- This little book helped me keep things in perspective.

My Stroke of Insight by Jill Bolte Taylor
- I could relate to her story about losing brain capacity, and I didn't feel alone.

Journals

I kept various journals around my house and wrote in them whenever inspiration struck or I needed to express something. They served as memory aids for me. It wasn't just about recording the date, but also the moment. Writing in these journals helped me transition from just speaking into my phone to capturing my thoughts on paper, allowing me to relearn and rebuild my cognitive abilities.

Painting

I remember the longing to reconnect with my creative side. At first, it wasn't about sharing with others or having an audience; it was about finding a space where I could immerse myself in an activity—something that sparked an, "Oh yes, I want to do that" feeling. It allowed me the freedom to paint whatever emotions I was experiencing. This became a vital medium for self-expression when I needed it the most.

During that period, I was still recovering physically and mentally, but this creative outlet offered a unique way to express myself. It provided not just an activity but also a sense of purpose. I distinctly remember searching for something I could manage, which was crucial for my recovery. It motivated me to get up and, at times, relearn simple tasks like navigating downstairs and remembering where things were. Seeing my work served as a catalyst, inspiring me to express myself in new and different ways.

Have one large, blank canvas for friends to paint.
I started with a huge canvas and invited my friends to add their own special touches with paints. Each would add new dimensions to the artwork. Some friends would sit there and paint multiple times, truly expressing themselves. When I look at it now, it feels like a big, comforting hug—a representation of my recovery. For friends who struggle to find the right words, painting offered a way to express their emotions. I didn't want to go through this process alone, and the painting serves as a reminder that I have support.

BODY

Some days were dedicated to building back my physical strength, while others focused on mental clarity. I discovered that repairing my body and healing my mind required intense focus but demanded different types of energy. Waking up and walking was hard, but, despite the pain, I got up. Each step to the bathroom was a small win, a reminder of my limits and progress. It was humbling! Each day, I celebrated small wins: walking a bit farther, standing a bit longer, and taking care of myself more easily. Here are some ways that I rebuilt my body:

Get out of bed.
- It might sound simple, but there were days that I didn't want to move. So, try to get up—making the bed not required.

Ask yourself, "How do I feel today?"

- By paying close attention to how you feel, you can gauge your capabilities and adjust accordingly.

Short walks with a purpose.

- I would take my dog, Teddy, for short walks, and she looked forward to them.

Gentle yoga.

- Walking to yoga was a huge step. The class was at a specific time, and I had to make sure that I get there by walking before the class started.

Sound meditation.

- In sound meditation, I would just sit in the same position for 45 minutes and let the vibration of sound be a part of my recovery.

Work with a trainer.

- I hired a trainer to help me rebuild my strength. It was a financial commitment, but it made me show up.

SPIRIT

To me, our spirit is the centerpiece of where we exist and how we are connected to others. It's not physical, it's spiritual. It's not from the brain, it's from the heart. While each of us carries our unique soul, a reflection of our inner peace and centeredness, we remain intrinsically connected to one another. This is how I physically connected to my spiritual guides and higher wisdom.

Intuitive Cards

I have a stack of different cards, and every morning I would pick a deck. I couldn't read when I first started, so I just looked at the artwork. This process helped me to read again.

I'd pick a card or select something meaningful and leave it out as my personal sign for the day. Here are the cards I used:

Rumi Oracle: An Invitation into the Heart of the Divine by Alana Fairchild

- The artwork on these cards is beautiful, and I just loved looking at them and feeling what I felt.

Medicine Cards: Discover the Power Through the Ways of Animals by Jamie Sams and David Carson

- I would pick a card, then I would read what it meant in the book companion.

Health, and the Law of Attraction cards: The Teachings of Abraham by Esther Hicks and Jerry Hicks

- These cards focus on your body-mind connection. Each day I would pull at card to remember how much control my mind had on my body and its recovery.

Well-Being Cards by Esther and Jerry Hicks

- Each of the bright and happy cards is an inspirational piece of wisdom, and they helped elevate my state of well-being.

Along with the cards, I listened to Dr. Joe Dispenza's meditations (drjoedispenza.com) about connecting to the universe and the quantum field.

FOR CAREGIVERS

I've been fortunate to have a tight group of friends who stood by me through everything, including wiping my ass. However, it's also true that some people, despite their love for me, found it too difficult to stay connected to me because they couldn't handle the weight of my trauma. This doesn't diminish their care or our connection; it simply means that everyone has different capacities for dealing with such

"Understanding and empathy are key. Recognize that everyone copes with trauma differently, and while some might not be able to stay close, their love and care are still valid."

— Shannon Michelle

intense situations. That took me a while to figure out, and I went through some dark nights trying to understand why a few of my closest friends ghosted me.

Sometimes I had to tell my friends to "shut the fuck up" if I couldn't handle knowing or understanding the stories they wanted to tell me about me or my accident. Do whatever you need to prevent pain for yourself; please don't be fearful or ashamed to share that.

I spoke to the friends who stood by me, and these are the things that kept them going through their personal trauma:

- Read: *It's OK That You're Not OK* by Megan Devine.
- Find your support system.
- Call or text a friend. Relying on each other through those difficult moments may be crucial.
- Go hiking; get out in nature.
- Join a group for caregivers in your local community or online.

For more resources, visit **StepIntoYourMiracle.com**

about
the author

Celebrated as one of Los Angeles' top interior designers, Shannon lived at the peak of luxury and creative fulfillment, curating spaces for A-list clients while traveling the globe and enjoying her success. But her life took a drastic turn when a near-death experience destroyed her mind and body, forcing her to confront the deepest truths about her priorities and the way she had been living.

After her near-death experience and waking from a coma, Shannon embarked on a challenging recovery from a traumatic brain injury and multiple life-threatening injuries. She had to relearn everything—how to move, think, and live. A battle with breast cancer further tested her world, but through these hardships, she unearthed an extraordinary resilience.

Recognizing that material achievements are not as significant as the value of authentic connections and inner fulfillment, Shannon left behind the glitz and glamour she once knew. Today, she is a sought-after speaker and author, sharing her powerful story and the tools she cultivated through immense hardship.

Shannon's voice is one of serene strength and compassionate wisdom. Her message, shaped by her experiences, is a beacon for those facing physical, emotional, or spiritual challenges. Shannon empowers others to live fully, authentically, and with purpose.

I'd love to hear how this book has inspired you! Please don't hesitate to drop me an email at **shannon@StepIntoYourMiracle.com** *and share your story with me. Let's connect and continue this amazing journey together. I'll let you know where I'll be speaking, and maybe we can catch up over a cup of tea.*

Much love,
Shannon Michelle

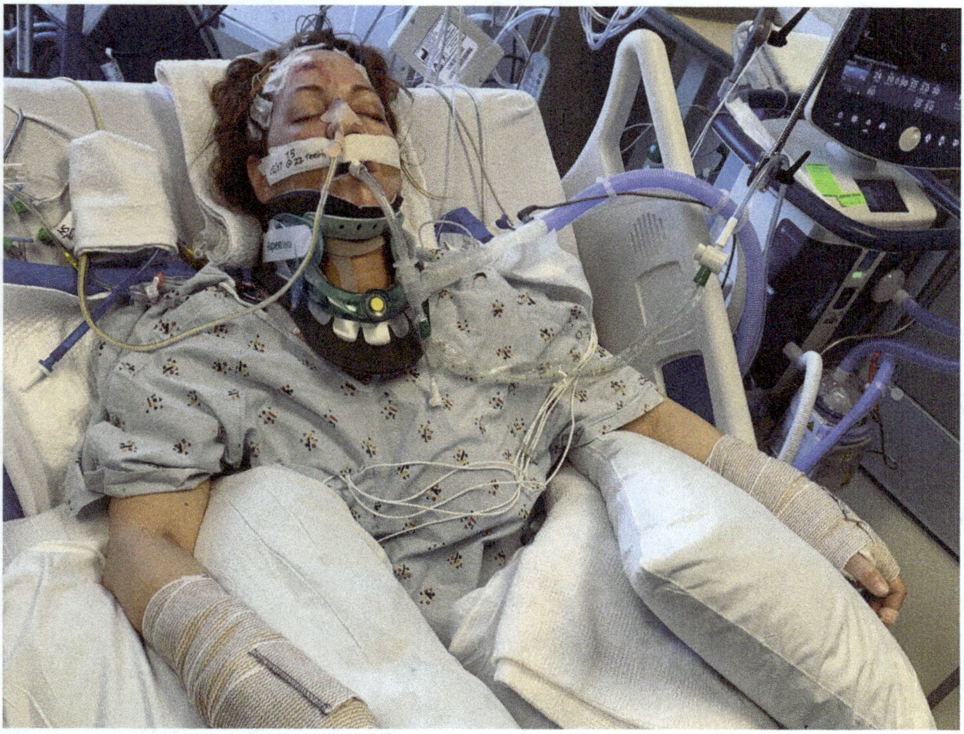

Shannon in a coma at UCLA

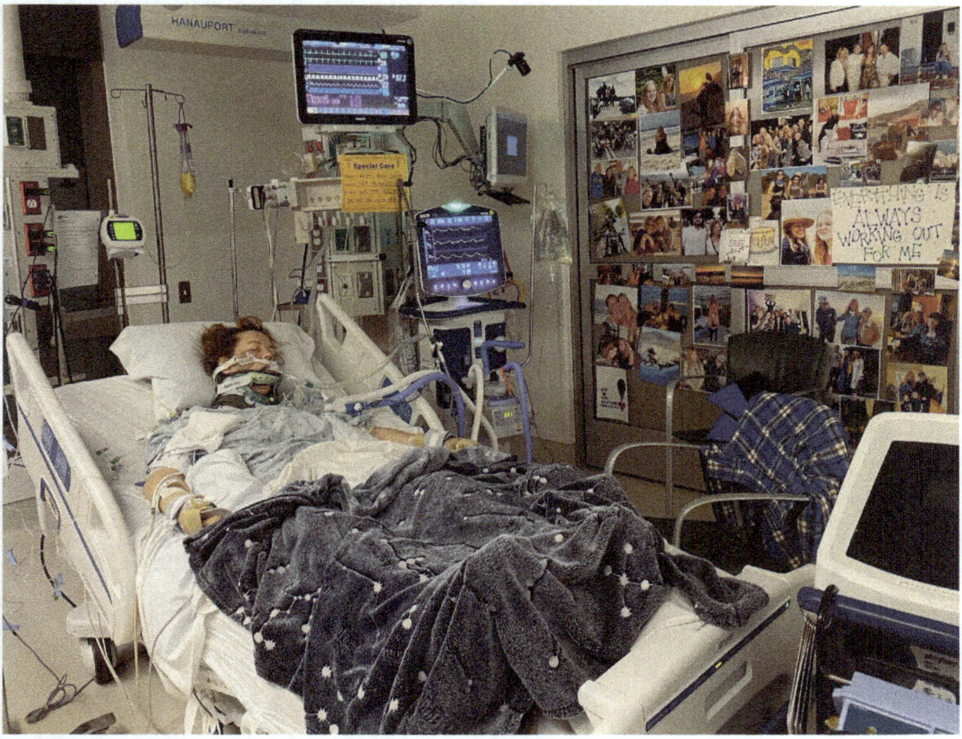

Twenty days after the accident

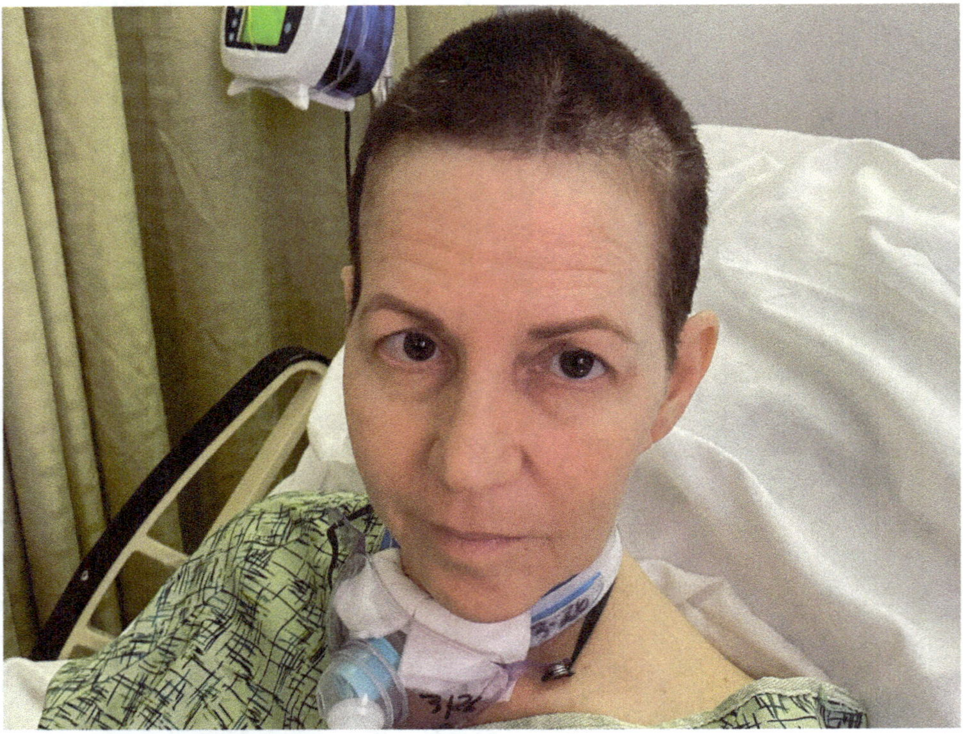

Head shaved and breathing assistance through a "trach" tube.

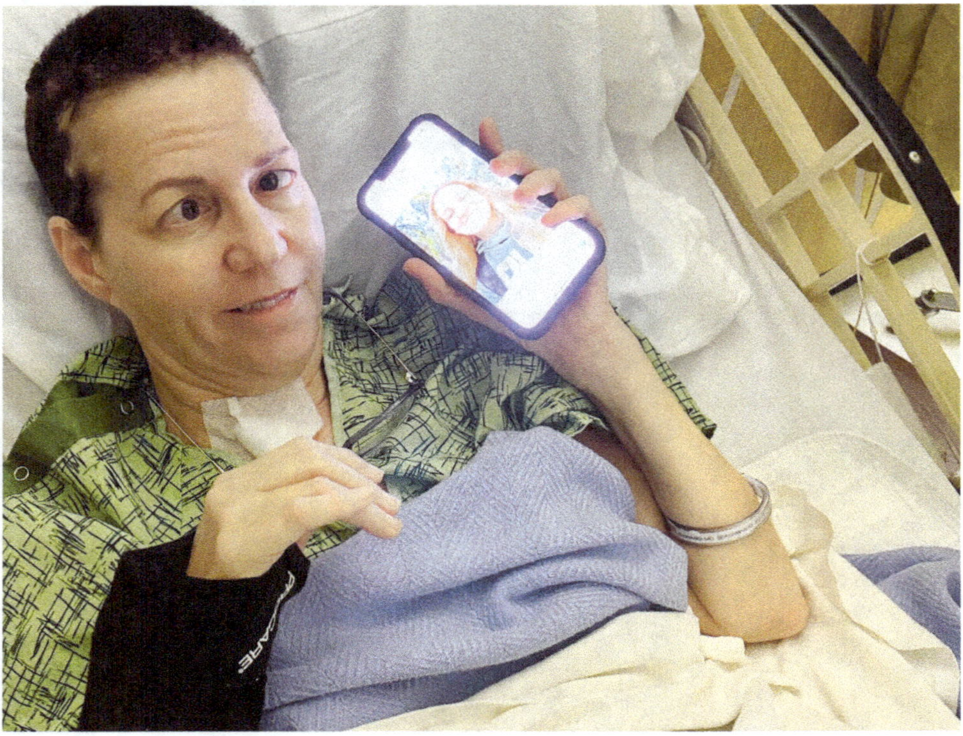

Tracheostomy removed

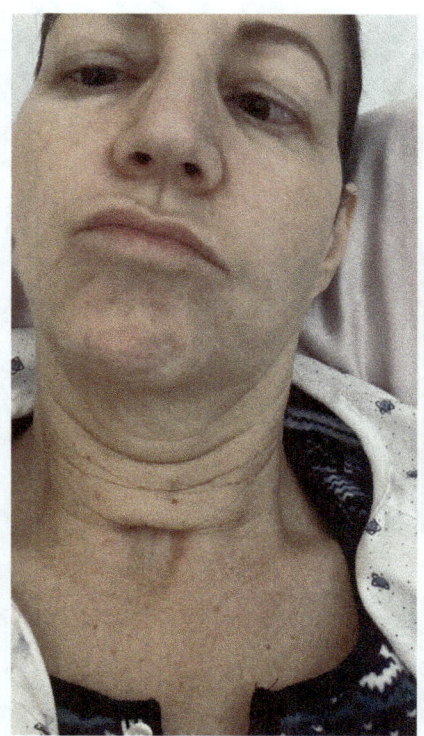

Painful trach scar

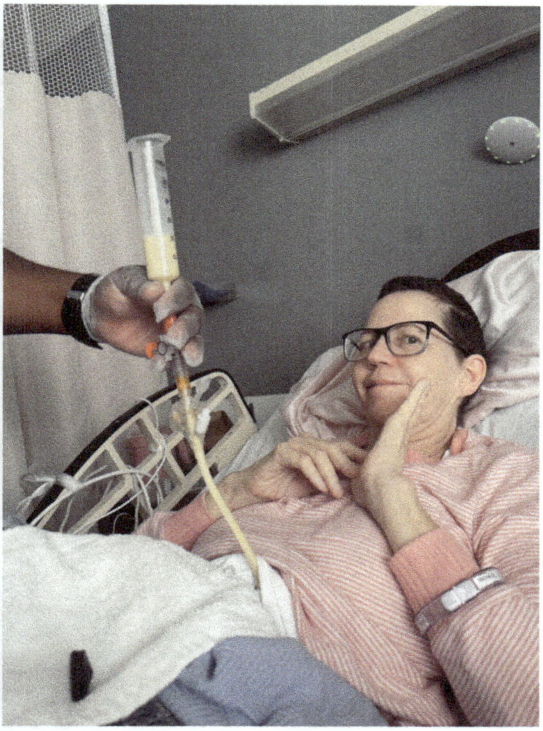

Feeding tube

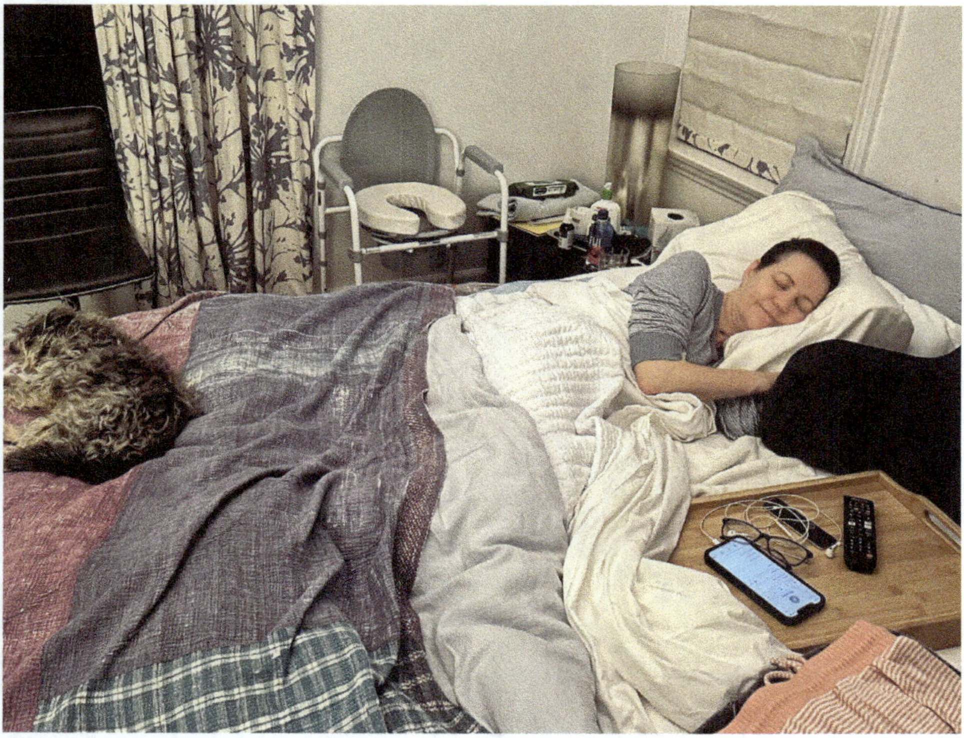

Back home with Teddy

Shannon and Grace, July 19, 2021

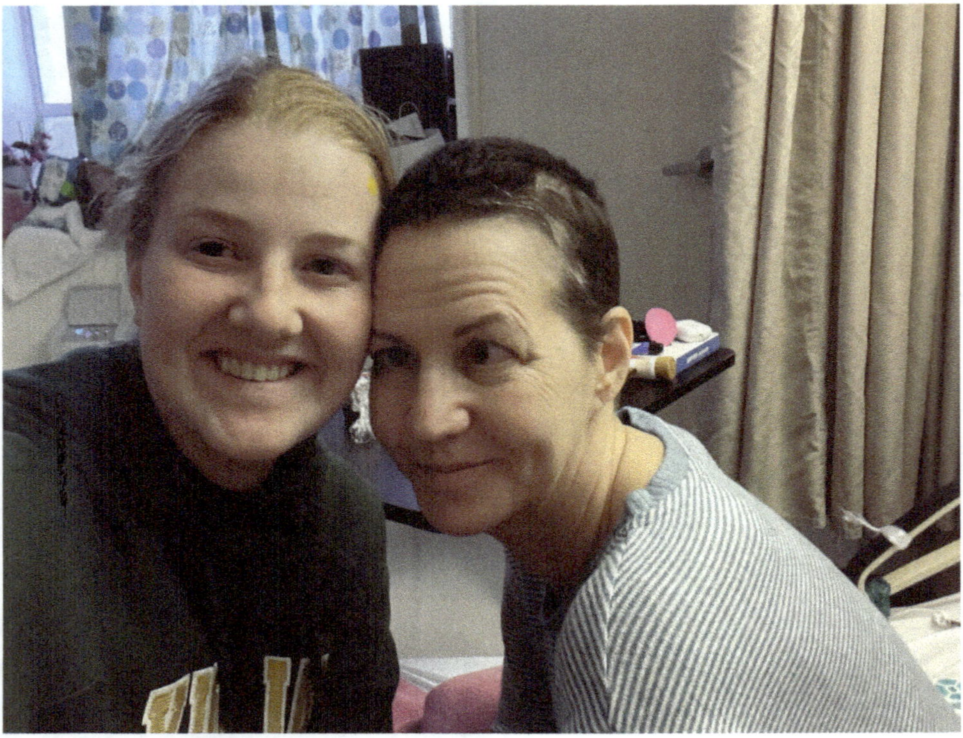

Shannon and Grace, April 22, 2022